People Tactics

Become the Ultimate People Person:

Strategies to Navigate Delicate Situations, Communicate Effectively, and Win Anyone Over

By Patrick King, Social Interaction Specialist at
www.PatrickKingConsulting.com

D1277632

Table of Contents

Introduction

In my opinion, one of the greatest movies in existence is *Back to the Future* – specifically the first of the trilogy, though the third edition shouldn't be discounted.

And we can just forget the second movie ever happened, but I digress.

It's no secret among my friends that I love the movie, and that I have semi-serious aspirations to purchase a DeLorean some day.

Disappointingly, this story is not about my fondness for all things 1980's.

A friend was hosting a dinner party that was a loosely veiled front for a matchmaking event – each friend had to bring a single friend of the opposite sex.

Sounds like the potential for a good night, right?

All went well until I met Dorothy. She was pleasant at first, but when I happened to mention my opinion on *Back to the Future*, things turned sour. She made a face as if she had smelled a dirty diaper and proceeded to give me her opinion on *Back to the Future*, her theories on time travel, and every inconsequential plot hole in the movie.

Did you know that Michael J. Fox wasn't even the original actor cast for Marty McFly? He wasn't that great anyway.

Why didn't the characters just tell the truth to each other?

Why was Marty's mom was attracted to her own son?

And so on.

After her monologue on the movie, it was clear her conclusion was that the movie was terrible and that I should feel bad for liking it. Even after I tried to walk away from the conversation turned lecture, she cornered me by the pizza rolls later that night and tried to re-state her points.

I remember thinking at that point how she was one of the most annoying people I had ever met, but it wasn't until later that I was able to articulate why.

She was a full-blown, card-carrying member of the *Belief Police*. She was the person that would track you down just to tell you that you were wrong.

In these people's minds, it's unfathomable that people can have different beliefs and think differently from them. They can't stand the fact that you disagree with their perspective or come to a different conclusion, and they attempt to patrol your brain for disagreeable beliefs and thoughts.

These are the same people who will tell you that things based on your opinion or tastes are just plain wrong. They aren't malicious, but this behavior comes from a stunning lack of self-awareness.

Awareness, openness, and listening are all cornerstones of becoming the consummate people person – the person in the room that can handle any situation and always knows how to react.

These are teachable concepts, and though you might not be a member of the Belief Police, it's often the smaller, more nuanced signals we send out that repel people, or make us less trustworthy and liked.

You can call them interpersonal skills, people skills, or just how to get along with anyone.

I prefer *People Tactics* because you never know how you might need to duck, dodge, and covertly handle people!

I want to teach you the most important aspects of connecting with others and understanding them as a means to the action you want. Some of them seem counterintuitive, common sensical, or too nuanced to matter – but that's the thing, they do matter, and it's people's tendencies to completely ignore them that leads to an interrogation over pizza rolls.

For the record, she didn't change my opinion on *Back to the*

Future.

Chapter 1. Take Ownership and Responsibility

Traveling: the more you do it, the more you love it. Or hate it – because of the realities of traveler's diarrhea and the jet lag that comes with shifting time zones.

If you're traveling with a friend, this can cause you to act in one of two ways.

If you know they love to plan and have a bionic map functioning inside their brains, you will probably relax and blindly follow them. You might feel free to kick your feet up and trust that they know what they are doing.

On the other hand, if you know and are aware that your friend is rubbish with a map and can't navigate his way out of a paper bag, you might approach your trip far differently.

What's the articulable difference?

You'd take ownership.

You would take it upon yourself to be accountable for what happens during the trip because no one else would. You'd approach the trip far differently, and check every box required to make sure it went smoothly.

Here's an example of ownership in action.

Suppose two people move to a new city. One decides to actively meet new people, and makes a point of being proactive about seeking out events to attend and activities to participate in. The other goes to work, and then goes straight home afterward, all the while wondering why he can't meet new people.

What's the difference? The degree of responsibility and ownership.

Guess what? It's the same with your interpersonal skills and people. You can't assume that others are going to help you out and make interactions go smoothly or even comfortably.

If you're failing, people won't bend over backwards to help you remedy a situation or solve a conflict for you. You need to accept responsibility for your interpersonal interactions. That is the first step toward improving them.

When you do this, you'll think about them beforehand, prepare for them, and proceed to bite your nails until you're sure they are good. This very natural level of anxiety combined with forethought is the secret and often overlooked foundation of amazing skills in any aspect of life.

Most people have the tendency to blame others for their failings and shortcomings. In social and interpersonal terms, doing this causes you to make excuses and mutter things like, "Wow, they were so weird and boring and hard to talk to" or "What was wrong with them" instead of looking in the mirror at yourself and wondering what you could have done better.

One of the biggest obstacles to learning is the tendency to blame other people for your successes and failures. Doing so exempts you from responsibility and thus the ability to look at your own actions honestly so that you can improve. Overall, it's a bad pattern for approaching your life and your interactions.

If you're too quick to pass the blame or shift accountability, it's going to be extremely hard to connect with people the way you want. The key to constant and consistent improvement of interpersonal skills is to hold yourself accountable for the process. This way, you put yourself in a position to constantly adjust, modify, and learn.

Only a tiny fraction of the people you meet have excellent people and interpersonal skills. They weren't born that way. These individuals learned to deal with people on an incredibly high level to produce the positive outcomes they enjoy. They almost certainly took ownership of these skills to intentionally cultivate them.

What does the opposite look like?

Hopefully, it doesn't sound too familiar: instead of directly taking action on your life, you assume the role of a passive audience member and view your life from that vantage point. It's as if you're watching the movie of your life and there's really nothing you can do besides watch the scenes play out according to a script you didn't write. You're just stuck in your seat as things happen to you; you can't take action and make things happen. You are powerless and helpless.

Of course, many people do this so they can ignore responsibility for their negative failings and keep their self-esteem intact. For example, if you can blame a tense and awkward conversation on others, then you're not at fault and you can keep your positive self-perception pristine and clear.

It doesn't matter whether the other person is being cranky or whether the other person seems like they just have it out for you. You need to take ownership of creating a good relationship, interaction, or other interpersonal situation.

What matters is how you choose to respond to the external stimuli life throws your way. If this is how you approach things, your chances of producing positive outcomes increase tremendously. You put yourself in a position where you can take action to make things turn out for the better.

You have to make your own luck in the social realm; you cannot just sit back and hope you'll get lucky.

Step one – picking up this book! You've realized that you can't rely on luck as a factor in your interpersonal success, so you have already taken the first step by proactively looking for and finding methods for a higher likelihood of success.

How often are you going to be able to say something like, "Oh my, God! You were born in the same tiny town I was and we shared babysitters as children!?" Situations like that are far and few between so we often have to manufacture interactions.

The added bonus of realizing you need to take ownership of situations is that you will prepare for all the contingencies you would not have thought about if you were placing responsibility on other people. You'll develop the habit of paying attention to small details and nuances in your interpersonal interactions that will allow you to be more interesting and charming.

What if they say this, what if they do that, what if I sneeze and spill my drink all over them?

There's a large difference between being reasonably worried about an upcoming meeting or interview, and obsessing about all the possibilities for hours because you feel as if you have to. With enough thought, we can often predict the direction a conversation or interaction will take. Being at least somewhat familiar with the possibilities and being prepared for them can be transformative.

Don't just expect the other side to pick up the slack. You can't expect the world to open the door for you. You have to open it yourself, and you have to proactively step through it.

Suppose you are on a rowboat with a man who only has one arm. Who might you expect to do the rowing?

Pretend that everyone you speak to only has one arm in the interaction. Don't expect any help and you'll be prepared when you don't receive any, and happily surprised and grateful when you do.

The bottom line is you have to take control over the *whole* process. Nobody's going to do it for you. Pretend that there is an invisible gas tank that represents each social interaction you have. You are responsible for filling 100% of it.

Resolve to start behaving differently tomorrow compared to the template that you're already working with today, because obviously that template is not giving you the kind of results you want.

This book spells out the process by which you can take your social interaction skills to the next level. However, in order for the tips in this book to be valuable to you, you have to start with the most basic – *you have to take ownership for them.*

Start with asking yourself these questions about ownership in regards to your interpersonal skills:

- Why did my last interaction go so poorly?
- What could I have done better?
- What were the possible signals I sent that made the other person react negatively?
- How can I alter my behavior going forward?

Chapter 2. Find Secondary Self-Interests

Getting along better with people doesn't just mean that you are more likable.

Getting along better with people means that you *appear* to understand them on a deeper level; that you "get" them and their motivations – even if you don't.

If you aren't able to achieve this level of understanding, you'll probably get more cold reactions than warm ones.

This is why we play the "Where are you from?" game and the "Oh! I spent some time there. Do you happen to know Joe Johnson?" game. We are innately seeking ways to imply understanding of each other, as it is the fast track to rapport and getting along.

What is the secret to getting people to feel that you "get" them? It's not sneaky or underhanded and it isn't even difficult.

You just have to take a split second to think about their self-interest, and how they stand to benefit by an action, event, or statement.

Human beings are motivated by self-interest, whether we want to admit it or not. A lot of us talk a big game regarding altruism, but deep down we have a fairly narrow range of self-interests. If you are completely honest with yourself, you will see that a lot of the seemingly altruistic stuff you do is actually selfish to some degree.

That's not necessarily a negative, though. Without self-interest, the world would be an unpredictable mess. With it, people become much more predictable and act in patterns.

Self-interest allows you to read this book – someone designed the computer or e-reader tablet out of self-interest, and Amazon sells products out of self-interest – even though others benefit.

The world runs on self-interest. Wrap your mind around this concept, otherwise it's too easy to fall into the common trap of thinking that self-interest is bad or inherently selfish. If approached properly within the social sphere, self-interest produces a win-win situation that leaves all parties involved satisfied and happy.

Actively Think Win-Win

Now that you have a clear idea of the importance of self-interest, the next step is to let it inform your social interactions.

When you approach people in social situations, actively think about creating a win-win situation by satisfying their self-interest.

You win because you've satisfied your purpose in speaking and connecting with them; they win because you paid attention to their interests and added value to them.

Even if you're not asking for anything, you will simply get more of what you want because you will address what's important to them and will have given them what they are looking for.

For example, if you approach a stranger at a networking event, a good strategy is to (1) determine their self-interest, and (2) deliver a win-win interaction by asking what they want to get out of the event.

Very often, they want to make high level contacts or secure new business. Supposing this is the case, you could help them brainstorm about whom to meet and contact, and then you could help by introducing them around or engaging others in group small talk. You gain a new friend and ally, and they see their wallet swell.

Other self-interests in a social setting are not related to goals at all: connecting with someone, meeting a good listener, feeling validated, making someone laugh, sharing about themselves – these are the real daily self-interests that you can help people achieve.

When you come to more structured settings such as the

workplace, self-interests become even more important because you will constantly run into either conflict or a situation where one person wins at the expense of others. There usually isn't enough figurative pie for everyone to eat their fill in an office environment and that creates bitterness or a clear win-lose situation.

An example of a win-win situation with self-interests would be where you and a co-worker are both attempting to look good in front of your boss.

The best way to look good in front of a supervisor is to engage with them, or work in a way that they can see your diligence. Obviously, there is limited face time available, so knowing your coworker's self-interest, you might help them look good in front of the boss in person, while you focus on sending diligent research and follow-up emails to show your worth. This is the same pie of your boss's attention, but you are feasting on the crust while allowing your coworker to feast on the strawberry filling.

Now suppose your coworker is exceedingly greedy and wants to block you at every turn. How can you make this into a win-win situation that doesn't feel as if you are just helping them sabotage you?

This is where you start to look at people's secondary self-interests.

That's the skill to develop and hone in this chapter. (1) If the primary pie is too small, what are the parts of the primary pie that people will enjoy? (2) What are the *secondary* pies that you can discover to keep all parties happy? Let's call these secondary self-interests, and they are what will really turn the tide in any interaction, whether friendly or adversarial.

Here, when you look to create win-win situations, you are looking to find other pies or give people the slice of pie they will most enjoy. Normally, when people compete, they always look to split a pie of resources in such a way that their slice is bigger and others have to lose out.

So besides the promotion at work, what else motivates your coworker? In other words, what besides securing that promotion will make them happy and how can you help them with that?

This is when you create another pie that only your coworker wants, so they can eat their fill without disturbing your self-interest. And even better, both sides still win.

This is another layer of analysis you can start developing for yourself – what are the other person's less-mentioned motivating factors? What else do they desire in this context, and what would make them happy? There will always be more than one goal or objective.

In the case of your coworker, what else drives them to be so aggressive in demanding your supervisor's time?

Is it a need for validation and recognition, insecurity, a crush on the boss, feeling alienated in the office, not having office friends, a lack of awareness, and an assumption that you don't like them?

Most of those are things you can easily address to satisfy their self-interest, which will naturally make them like you more and result in your getting along better.

People hate to lose or not get what they want. This is why too many people have a win-lose mindset. If you dig deep enough, you can find a way for them to feel as if they're winning with you, or better yet, *because* of you.

If you can properly identify and add value to others' self-interests, you can increase your charisma and how people perceive you. In many cases, that might be your only win, but it is a cumulative one with great cache.

The best part about this people tactic is that you can be fairly transparent about what you're trying to accomplish – helping their self-interests.

It's like when you are evaluating taking a new job. The primary self-interest might obviously be money and prestige, but those aren't the only things that matter for a new job. You are never making a decision in a vacuum, and that's where secondary interests come into play. *They might be secondary on paper, but they can often take precedence over primary interests.*

For example, with a new job, a shorter commute, a greater sense of community, an interesting work culture, working with people directly, or the great location might be more important than simple salary.

Pies, pies, pies.

It should rarely be the case where you both reach for the same slice of pie. And with the knowledge of this chapter, it should never happen again.

Chapter 3. The Anti-Golden Rule

The standard rule when it comes to interpersonal interaction is the Golden Rule. The Golden Rule is, of course, to treat others the way you want to be treated.

But should we?

I have a friend with a particularly dark sense of humor. Maybe dark isn't the right word – he just likes putting people into uncomfortable positions and cherishes when people do it right back to him. It's like a verbal staring contest.

I, on the other hand, coach people on how to avoid exactly these situations and have smooth conversations and better social fluency. You might imagine that the Golden Rule does not apply to interactions between him and me.

And in fact, it really shouldn't apply to interactions with most people. The Golden Rule sounds like a nice concept but really falls apart upon a closer look.

We all have different standards of good, bad, and acceptable. It's decidedly inefficient and plain weird when we try to apply a single standard, even if it is our own, to others.

The better way to approach others?

The Platinum Rule: Treat others how they want to be treated.

It sounds simple, but this mentality has the ability to transform your interactions.

The Golden Rule, for its positive intentions, is a self-centered way of viewing other people. When deciding how to act toward others, you aren't giving them a second thought. Instead, you are assuming that people are similar to you and think the same way; you are attributing or imposing your thoughts onto them. This assumes that you are a reasonable person with normal sensibilities, which also might not be the case.

It's why you so often hear things like, "Why are you so annoyed? You know I was joking. That's just my sense of humor!" Yes, and you expected other people to either conform or innately understand you.

One of the keys to being better with people and being better liked is to wipe the slate clean and assume that you don't know how others want to be treated. When you start viewing people from their own perspective, instead of your own, you will get better results.

Suppose you are rich and are giving your friend Jonathan a present at his birthday party. Since you like rich, lavish gifts, you might assume that Jonathan does as well. But Jonathan is decidedly conservative with money, and lives in a poor neighborhood where things are stolen frequently.

In this case, treating someone the way you wish to be treated doesn't make the most sense, and also doesn't serve that person well.

We're all wearing blinders that are made from our self-interests, past experiences, and backgrounds.

Unfortunately, our blinders can sometimes be strapped so tightly that we start looking at all the other people around us as extensions of ourselves. We start looking at situations as opportunities to advance our own agendas instead of simply taking a step back and asking what someone else might think about it.

The Golden Rule embodies another problem: what if you don't respect yourself very much?

What if you have a poor opinion of yourself, and don't take care of yourself mentally or physically? What if you believe that the world is cruel and no one deserves any sympathy or help? This would be a poor mentality to carry over to others.

The Platinum rule produces much better results because you are forced to step into other people's shoes.

Want to be a better people person?

How about more trustworthy?

Or just be more highly regarded?

Take the focus off of yourself and free yourself from self-absorption. Apply the Platinum Rule and force yourself to think externally and outwardly.

If you're having difficulty connecting with others, understanding them, or just making small talk, this is probably your biggest shortcoming. You're probably subconsciously thinking "What can I get out of this conversation?" and while that line of thinking can occasionally be practical and positive, it's not conducive to growing interpersonal skills.

The better approach is to think, "What is going on in this person's life, where are they coming from, and based on an educated guess, how would they like to be treated?"

It's a bit more of a mouthful, but it becomes second nature after you practice it.

We all have different contexts and we all have different settings. Some people respond differently depending on the company they keep. Other people behave differently based on location. By thinking in terms of the Platinum Rule, you pay close attention to these nuances. You are able to then predict the best approach to speaking and interacting with people.

By doing this, you will finally let go of the "One size fits all" social template that you have previously been using. Best of all, putting yourself in other people's shoes more often helps you develop a sense of empathy and perspective that you may never have had before. This is a relatively rare skill. It will enable you to stand out in any kind of social situation and make your social value more apparent.

For example, there is a new parent in your office. You are young, unmarried, and without a child. When you engage them, you have zero interest in talking about children. The Golden Rule would direct you away from the topic of children, but the Platinum Rule would ask what they would want to talk about. Guess what? It would be children.

One of the most valuable exercises for developing this kind of empathy is to read fiction and articulate exactly what the characters are feeling and why. This allows you to completely ignore yourself because you're a character, and focus on the nuanced desires of people. If the book is well-written, you might be able to predict the plot from a combination of the personalities of the characters + the plot turns.

John spurns Mary, and Mary has a history of constant rejection. What do you think the fallout will be, and will John feel guilty or laugh about it?

We've covered how people are driven by self-interest. We're subconsciously thinking about the value people provide them.

People persons actively think about what is in it for the

other side of the party. Consciously attempt to look at your conversation with another person from their perspective. Based on what you know about their history and their identity, you can throw out many of the "filler" questions and get straight to how they like to be treated.

For example, if you know someone is relatively negative and complaint-oriented, you wouldn't waste time talking about the every day miracle of the sun rising. That's not what they're interested in, and not how they enjoy engaging with others. Relate to them with relatable negative aspects of life or your current setting. They can be as benign as possible, but that's the tone they are accustomed to thinking in. You've just found how they like to be treated.

If you're in a poor mood, you might want to be uplifted with kitten videos, but the same wouldn't hold for our negative friend.

This is a key step to becoming a better conversationalist and interpersonal master.

In some respect, this chapter might seem like it just tells you to ignore your own desires and turn yourself into a puppet for other people.

In a sense, that's true.

People will always respond better to things they can relate to or that are about them. But it's not manipulative or pandering to take advantage of that knowledge. Instead, it shows people that you're different, and that there are easier roads into people's hearts.

Remember, this book is about focusing on the goal of becoming a better people person. "Just be yourself" isn't always the best way to accomplish that goal. Once you cross the threshold and can easily build rapport with strangers, you can interweave your own approach with the Platinum Rule.

It turns out that, in many respects, salespeople have it right. If you want to sell a product, you'd better learn about your target audience and then speak in a way that appeals to them and makes their ears perk up.

The Platinum Rule applies in all social settings as well as in conversations. You'd be surprised as to what you would see if you chose to borrow other people's eyes and ears.

Chapter 4. Reform Toxic Habits

One of my best friends never knows when to shut up.

Most of the time I enjoy this about him because he usually has something insightful or hilarious to say. He is forever a source of entertainment because he has no reservations about poking fun at every aspect of himself. He might be the most shameless person I know.

He isn't, however, a great listener.

This is showcased mostly when I want to rant about something inane that happened during my day, such as a driver cutting me off, or the market running out of my favorite kind of donuts (maple glazed) before I could get there.

The only purpose for those rants is to burn off some of my annoyance so it doesn't affect the rest of my day. It doesn't take long, and I'm not screaming or pounding the table.

Despite all this, he just *has* to interject immediately and try to solve the problem. For example, if I am indeed complaining about the absence of donuts, he'll immediately ask me what I can do about it, and suggest five actions for me to take to find the donuts from either their source, or petition the market to fry more in the afternoons.

I can appreciate the gesture, but it's downright annoying when I can't finish my thought without hearing suggestions that I will never use and barely care about. Sometimes you just want to gripe a little and be heard; you are not actually looking for advice or even a solution.

Despite how great a person you might be, you probably have toxic habits that repel people instead of attract them, and really, make you an anti-people person.

If "just be yourself" hasn't been working for you, then perhaps it's because "yourself" is grating, lacks tact, and doesn't play well with others. You just might have some habits that are blocking your path to greater success in all areas of your life.

There's always room for improvement, and you have to be open to letting go of some key traits that you think make up who you are.

Bad Habit #1: You are never fully present.

When you're talking with other people, you give out the impression that you'd rather be somewhere else, with someone else.

You think in the back of your mind that other people simply are not that interesting. To put it bluntly, you think most other people are boring. It's bad enough that you think these things, but then you make it worse by telegraphing your feelings through your body language and your use of eye contact.

When people look at you, they can easily tell that you are not interested and in turn will think you not a nice person to be around. At best, you make people feel you simply don't care about them. At worst, you can come off as somebody who's flat out hostile.

And you know what? It's your fault for not valuing the person in front of you enough to make an effort.

Quick Fix

The quick fix to this bad habit is to admit that this is your fault.

If you think you're having a boring conversation that you want to get away from, you have to admit that you caused the problem. You caused the conversation to be boring because you expected it to be interesting, and you expected to be entertained by the other person instead of creating a conversation together.

How much work did you want to put in?

You had a sense of entitlement, and because of your disengagement, the other person also got nothing out of the interaction.

The fix here is to realize, appreciate, and understand that it's your job to make the conversation interesting. It's your responsibility. Pretend that you are a talk show host and ask questions about them to figure out why they do the things they do. Ask questions about the opinions they hold. Make it your goal to find common ground or an interesting tidbit about their life.

This is only possible if you have a sense of curiosity about other people. And if you don't have a natural sense of curiosity about what goes on in other people's lives, fake it.

Think of people you've wanted to meet since forever. What kind of questions would you ask them? Let people become aware of your sense of curiosity and energy and they will reciprocate.

Bad Habit #2: Your world is black and white.

Put another way, you only see one correct way of doing things, and anything that diverges from that view is wrong.

And that way happens to be your view.

This habit is particularly toxic because people who have this mindset are very judgmental. When they come across people that don't fit the mold of how they feel the world should operate, they judge them, sometimes to their faces. They are prone to thinking of that person as someone who is wrong, and can only respond in a very stereotypical way.

Just as you wouldn't want to be put in a box the moment

you talk to people, they also don't respond all that well to feeling as if they're being judged. This is a hard habit to break because opinions can easily become personal.

Unfortunately, our natural selfishness tends to translate to a black and white view in such a way that when our opinions are questioned, we ourselves feel judged and attacked. So people stop opening up to you, and will eventually avoid you altogether.

If somebody has an opinion, respect that opinion. Ask questions about how they came up with that opinion, and what information and assumptions they hold.

Quick Fix

This black and white thinking is actually very easy to solve.

The vast majority of judgment comes from viewing yourself as superior to others. Therefore, the best way to undermine this toxic mindset is to consider alternative explanations to our judgmental statements.

Your grand explanation for something is just one possible conclusion that is neither better nor worse, just based on the information you have at your fingertips. Jog your creative faculties and try to understand how other people might have ended up with such a different opinion. Is their world view dramatically different from yours? What experiences have they had in their lives that might explain why they hold a position in such contrast to yours? Remember that people have their own reasons for opinions and beliefs and that not everybody thinks just the way you do.

Allow yourself to be curious as to how they reached their conclusion. Get excited about the story behind everyone and everything. Also recognize that judgment often comes from insecurity, jealousy, or resentment.

Bad Habit #3: You are a conversational narcissist and dominate conversations.

Some people are just in love with the sound of their voices.

They don't listen; they simply wait until the other person stops talking so they can start speaking again. They view the time during which another person is talking as a resting period for their vocal cords.

They don't acknowledge what others say. They don't even ask how the other person is doing. When people talk this way, it's because they find themselves more fascinating than the other people around them. It is extremely selfish and shows a deep and profound lack of interest in what drives, motivates, and interests other people.

Don't be the person who takes others hostage by talking their ears off.

Quick Fix

Thankfully, there is a quick fix to this narcissistic conversational mindset.

Impose a limit on yourself.

For example, for every story you share, you must ask the other person two questions about the story, or about things that are important to them. Keep track internally of how self-centered you are with regards to the topics you choose to talk about.

Challenge yourself to make your conversation a game to find out as much about other people as you can while saying as little as possible about yourself or the things you find interesting. Realize that people only feel good about and enjoy a conversation when they are sharing – you feel the same way.

Allow others to feel good by giving them time and space to talk about what's important to them. Otherwise, people will start avoiding you because they will think of you as someone who doesn't care. They might already have started to.

This narcissistic conversational habit comes from a place of insecurity and a need to prove oneself. It can get boring quite quickly. Give others air space and know that the inclination to prove oneself immediately is a dead giveaway for insecurity.

Bad Habit #4: You give unsolicited advice or opinions.

This is my best friend to a tee.

Many times, people just want to talk about something and think out loud. They're not looking to debate, realize something profound, hear advice, or act on anything. They just want to be heard and validated in a comfortable setting. In many cases, they just want to get a weight off of their chest and share feelings.

And that's it. That's all they're looking for. If people want advice, they'll ask.

You must be able to read people so you don't immediately turn them off by ignoring these central facts. When you give a response they were not looking for, people will begin to stay away from you.

Quick Fix

Take a moment to ascertain the purpose of a person's statement. Make it a binary choice: does this person actually want my input, or are they just letting off steam and need an ear to scream into? There is a big difference between the two.

If someone is asking for advice, let them ask specifically and explicitly. Otherwise, shut up. If they don't ask you for specific advice or specific solutions, be content with being a simple sounding board.

Allow people to spill their guts to you and they'll begin to trust you with other things as well.

Easy fix.

Bad Habit #5: You always need to be right.

There's an old saying, "I'd rather be happy than be right."

Probably made by a man in reference to marriage.

Unfortunately, a lot of people would prefer the opposite – to be right. They feel that they're coming off as weak if they give in. People like this always create excuses and rationalizations if anyone seeks to invalidate any part of their arguments or statements.

They have a stunning lack of vulnerability, and it's extremely infuriating to speak with somebody with this mindset. It should be easy to see why. If you don't see it, you just might be this person.

This person doesn't make you feel as if you're having a dialogue. Everything turns into a black or white debate or argument.

Every interaction has to produce a winner and a loser. These people tend not to divulge anything personal or reveal any shortcomings because they feel doing so would undermine their perceived self, and because they are driven by extreme insecurity. They want to be seen as strong, and one way they feel they can make this happen is to be infallibly correct.

Quick Fix

First, you need to be aware that you're doing this.

Second, you need to be aware of why you're doing it. Let me cut to the chase, the reasons are actually quite simple. People who engage in this behavior are extremely insecure. They do this because they're trying to protect their ego and pride. They can't bear others seeing them as less than perfect.

There is no such thing as a perfect person. Trying to pretend that you are only makes you look ridiculous.

Third, learn to choose your battles. You can't simply blow up on every little argument you have with your friends. People will not take you seriously; remember the boy who cried wolf one too many times.

It's also important you realize that your perception is *your* reality. It's your fault if you're feeling attacked and judged all the time to the extent that you have to defend yourself. If this is the case, change your perception. There's no need for the unnecessary drama and negative fallout from your need to constantly be right.

Chapter 5. Question Your Assumptions

This is a story I've told before, but I find that it excellently illustrates the assumptions in our lives and why we should question them constantly.

I was assigned a parking spot at a new job, and in my second week, someone was parking in it every morning. I tried arriving earlier and earlier in the day to catch the culprit red-handed, but it took another couple of weeks because it seemed that this person woke up at the crack of dawn just to steal my spot.

What kind of sick person would do this intentionally? They must have been a real bastard, bitter at the world, or have held a huge grudge against me. I hated them.

I was fuming about this the whole time, and when I finally decided to get there at 5:00 AM one morning, I found the culprit.

It was the company custodian who barely understood my

greeting of "Hi, good morning, how are you?" He just nodded his head, grabbed his mop, and headed inside. It was clear to me that the whole notion of assigned parking spots would be lost on him, so I just went back to my car and napped until work started.

I was driven by the faulty assumption that whoever was parking in my spot was doing so maliciously. What was my assumption based on? No evidence of any kind, just a stab in the dark about intention. I should have questioned my assumptions before wasting hours of sleeping time to confront a kindly old man.

The way people behave is driven primarily by their assumptions and beliefs. So where do those assumptions and beliefs come from?

It's not always clear, and sometimes they come from nowhere at all. But it's important to be aware of what you assume when you interact with people.

For example, if someone is quiet and sitting in the corner, what assumptions would you make about them? Maybe they're shy, introverted, and socially awkward? Not exploring alternative possibilities to your assumptions, and not giving people the benefit of the doubt will cause you to act in a way that makes them indeed socially awkward.

One of the biggest reasons people's interpersonal skills suffer is because of this exact process. People will make split second judgments and assumptions about others from tiny actions and never think twice about how incorrect the basis for their conclusions might be.

They'll put you in a position to be misunderstood and misinterpreted, without your even knowing it.

The best way to face this is to remember that the majority of people possess a degree of reasonableness.

If that is your starting line, you'll have far fewer arguments because you will have to assume there is a reasonable basis for why people believe in certain things. If you assume that people base their arguments and form their opinions based on logic, then it follows that they must be relying on facts and information you are not aware of.

If you make assumptions that ignore or undermine their logical flow and information, you are more likely to engage in meaningless arguments where one of the parties eventually exclaims, "Wait... *that's* what you thought I meant?"

There are a few assumptions that are particularly harmful when left unchecked, and can have a profoundly negative impact on your social interactions. It's okay to labor under these assumptions, as long as you can also provide alternative explanations for the conclusions you have arrived at.

Fault Assumption #1: All parties know what we are talking about.

Are you even talking about the same thing? Or is there a fundamental disconnect that explains why there are such differences of opinion?

Faulty Assumption #2: We already know the other person's view and opinions of the situation.

Often, we think we know where someone is coming from, and why. How can that be true? Unless you explicitly ask, there's no way to know for certain how someone feels about something, and the reasoning that led them there.

Faulty Assumption #3: We are right, they are wrong.

When you come to a situation with this assumption, there's no way it's going to end well or peacefully. This position on your part is the very opposite of giving someone the benefit of the doubt. You are completely invalidating their position and line of reasoning right off the bat and assuming moral and mental superiority.

Faulty Assumption #4: Everyone has the same set of facts.

This is similar to faulty assumption #1, except it assumes that if everyone were to have all the facts, the same conclusion would be drawn by all. It's an assumption that everyone has the same logic and makes the same mental leaps you do.

Do you have any of these quick assumptions? When you believe these, you put people into boxes and make interactions more tense or adversarial than they need to be. The better approach is to focus more on being curious and interested in what the other person knows and what facts have led them to their conclusion.

This way, the conversation is not reduced to a simple matter of black and white. Instead, you open yourself up to learning new facts that might change your opinion or strengthen it.

Here are a few more assumptions that can have a bigger impact than you might realize.

Assuming that Impact is the same as Intent

This is a particularly toxic assumption because you equate the bad effects of something with the intention of the person behind that action.

This is how I felt about the company custodian who kept stealing my parking spot.

Just because somebody did something bad does not necessarily mean that was their intent. In fact, with everything else being equal, this is almost never true. Unless you have solid facts to lead you to believe they intended the negative impact of their actions, jumping to that conclusion on your part will cause unnecessary animosity. Don't automatically conflate negative events with negative intentions or motives.

Assuming that you are as subtle or as obvious as you think

Just because you think something is subtle doesn't necessarily mean the person you're speaking with sees it the same way. You cannot assume that people understand your quirks and mannerisms.

Only people who have known you for a long time or who have observed you in a wide range of circumstances will be able to get into your head and accurately interpret you this way. Most of the time this will not be the case.

We only share "I was thinking that too!" moments with a few people, so when you assume that people will be able to pick up on your subtleties or your obvious statements, you are assuming too much. Don't give other people the responsibility of essentially reading your mind because they'll almost certainly read it incorrectly.

You simply cannot assume that people understand your secondary or even primary meanings. This is especially true when it comes to jokes, where it's easy to come across in the worst way possible. This is when you'll hear people exclaim things like *"OF COURSE I didn't mean it like that! How could I?"*

In many cases, you have to spell it out or do a better job of letting people know that you are joking.

Assuming that matters are personal

Just because something negative was said or proposed doesn't mean that it's a slight against you, or that there is a negative judgment about you. Often, these things are just observatory and people have much better things to do than fixate on your personal flaws.

You can begin to embody a victim mentality when you feel that everything is a personal affront. Then it becomes a self-fulfilling prophecy because others will start to avoid you and become frustrated with you – then you truly are the one suffering.

It's almost never personal and learning not to react with emotion is key here.

Learn to quell this handful of damaging assumptions and your charisma quotient will increase dramatically.

Chapter 6. Listen with Intent

As a general rule of thumb, I tend to listen far more than I speak. I do this because of a mixture of enjoying people's stories, and more important, I like to give others air space in a conversation.

In some order, here's what people enjoy about conversations. Being entertained, speaking and sharing, laughing, and learning something new.

Notice a pattern? If we aren't listening to something we feel has value to us, then we prefer to share about our lives and thoughts. Think about how you feel after you leave a conversation where you don't share much, and the air space was monopolized by the other person.

Your neck probably hurt from all that nodding and you felt as if you just left a lecture.

To become a people person, you need to listen way more than you speak. Since it's impossible that everything out of your mouth is going to be fascinating and compelling, let others share – they'll feel better about themselves and subsequently about you.

There's a giant caveat – to be a good listener, you aren't just giving air space and surrendering your turn to speak.

A lot of people think that to be a good listener, you just need to shut up and let the other person talk. While to some extent that's true, there are more parts to the puzzle. That's passive listening. To the other person, it can feel as if they are speaking to a wall.

Active listening is the key to giving others validation. It reads like a mouthful, but it's simple in practice. You are listening with intent.

Let's say that someone says, "Last weekend I was skiing but I wasn't really having a good time."

Passive listening would consist of you saying "Oh, cool" or "Uh huh" and only acknowledging their statement and staying silent afterward.

Active listening, and listening with intent, would consist of any of the following:

"Didn't have a good time…?"

(Repeating the last phrase of a person's statement) Or

"So, you went skiing but it wasn't the best time?"

(Rephrasing their statement back to them) Or

"Sounds like you were expecting a fun and active weekend but something was wrong or missing?"

(Sum up their thoughts and position)

When you read it from the page, it sounds like you might come off like a parrot or a robot. *Active listening is just repeating what someone says? How does that help?*

It helps because people hear far more than a repetition. They are hearing you use their own words in a new sentence, which gives the strong impression that you were listening intently. It appears that you are following their train of thought with interest. You want to make sure with crystal clarity that you understand them so you can delve deeper.

The best part of all this is the more you do this, the more they will continue to talk and take the conversation into deeper realms. You can literally mix the three types of phrases for an hour and observe in wonder as people pour their hearts out attempting to explain, justify, and elaborate.

The intent is to crack them open like a nut and learn as much about their inner thought process as possible.

This shows personal investment in the other person. People want to feel that they matter. People want to feel that what they have to say is something of consequence – that's the ultimate power of validation.

I wasn't sure whether or not I wanted to travel this summer.

Travel this summer?

Yeah, I was thinking about going to Greece but it might be too expensive.

You want to go to Greece minus the prices?

Yeah, I haven't traveled anywhere in the past few years and I've seen so many great pictures of the Greek Islands.

Sounds like you need to get away despite the cost!

You could be right. I mean, people are only young once, right? I've always dreamed of traveling the world but work gets in the way.

So work has always gotten in the way?

This conversation could probably continue *ad nauseum* ...but notice how all one party is doing is picking and choosing phrases to repeat so that the other party is beckoned to clarify and elaborate further?

It's no wonder that this is the exact technique that psychologists use during therapy sessions to allow people to discover themselves and articulate out loud their inner thoughts. A few well-placed questions in the form of active listening can really crack people open, as well as help them learn about themselves.

Match your tone of voice

Speaking of robots, you should use the exact opposite tone of voice. Where they are mechanic and unexpressive, you should tailor your tone of voice to be one of genuine curiosity and interest, as if you were asking "Did I get this right? Please correct me if I did not."

You may be able to master a curious tone of voice when you repeat a person's last three or four words, but you are only giving yourself away if your body language and facial expression give off the impression that you couldn't care less.

You have to remember that when you talk to people, you're not just communicating with the words coming out of your mouth. You're also communicating based on your body language, your facial expressions, and your gestures. If any of these run contrary to what you're verbally communicating, then you will come off as disingenuous and manipulative.

Make sure that you employ the correct body language and facial expression for effective and active listening. At the very least, this means constant eye contact and ample nodding. Engage and raise your eyebrows, smile genuinely and don't let your smile fade too quickly; maintain an open and relaxed body posture.

Your body language, in most cases, says it all. Either you're open to what this person has to say or you're simply nodding your head and saying reassuring stuff, but you've got your arms crossed. In other words, you'd rather be somewhere else.

React Sufficiently

When someone is sharing something with you, make sure you give off verbal and nonverbal signals that match the emotions they're trying to elicit.

In most cases, when people share or want to get stuff off their chest, they're looking for sympathy or a form of release. They're not going to get these if you are just going to sit there with a blank expression on your face.

They won't feel your assurances unless you make them explicit, because as we discussed, you can't assume they will understand your small signals.

So what are the most common kinds of emotions people are trying to elicit? It's usually excitement, shock, interest, or amusement. Keep these in mind and make sure to show them – it tells them their message is on point, well-received, and encourages them to share more.

When you listen more, you learn more about people and where they are coming from. You also learn more about their particular challenges in life. This enables you to fine tune your empathy skills. You will be able to recognize what they're dealing with. You will be able to figure out what they're happy and unhappy about. You will also learn about what worries them and what their cares are.

You will only get better at it the more you practice it.

Above all else, this skill set enables you to get into their world. The more you do this, the more you can view them as three-dimensional. We only judge those whom we know nothing about, so it also creates goodwill between you and others.

When you know more about people, you'll have more to ask about and genuinely care more about them. This paves the way for better and more meaningful interactions.

Chapter 7. Emotional Intelligence

Emotional intelligence has become somewhat of a buzzword the past few years, but most people don't quite know what it means.

Emotional intelligence is knowing what you feel and why you feel that way. You are able to put a label on your emotional state and find its cause and effect.

By extension, it's being able to read other people's emotions accurately and deduce the reasons for them.

When you start thinking "Why did she say that?" and "What made him do that?" that's the beginning of your path to emotional intelligence. Emotional intelligence is rooted in a natural curiosity about other people, so the more you care about others, the better you will get at it.

Why does any of this matter?

Emotionally intelligent people are less judgmental and more

empathetic because they understand other people's motivations and intentions and how that influences their emotions. In times of conflict, they can cut past emotional reactions and resist taking matters personally. In social situations, it means that people with high emotional intelligence can know exactly what to talk about and what excites or bores people.

High emotional intelligence is like being able to read someone's mind.

How do you gain this everyday superpower and increase your emotional intelligence?

The first step is to actively make an effort to know yourself better.

It's next to impossible to understand other people's thought patterns if you can't see your own with clarity. What follows sounds impossible, but you need to start thinking about how you think.

What you're really doing is taking a step back and pausing whenever you experience a strong emotion. Close your eyes and try to trace what happened in the past hour or two that led you to feel that way. Are there any facts or experiences in the past that would explain why you feel a particular way about certain things and people in your life?

You might be surprised by what you discover.

For example, if you're angry at 6pm, start thinking about what you've done since 3pm. You've driven home, had a snack, changed into your sweatpants, and watched a little bit of television.

When you visualize your drive home though, suddenly you remember that you were cut off by somebody and that you were beeped at incessantly. This agitated you and you were still feeling the effects of that mood dampener hours later. This is a simplification of the process that begins to take place much more instantly.

The sad reality is that most people are not in tune with their feelings.

Most people just react automatically without realizing why. They fall into patterns that are sometimes negative, and sometimes destructive.

Why do some people overeat? Because they're using food as therapy without realizing that they aren't hungry, just upset. Sometimes, nothing is more comforting than reacting in an automatic fashion. But that doesn't teach you anything about yourself.

Knowing yourself is probably the hardest job in the world. It's easier for us to judge other people than to actually take a long and honest look at how we feel and how we think.

The second step is to observe your actions.

Rather than looking inward and attempting to label your emotions based on what you might hypothesize caused them, analyze how you are acting and label them that way.

In the former, you are looking to the past to try to deduce a cause. In the latter, you are looking at the present to see the manifestation of emotion.

Just as with other people, you can tell more about yourself by your actions than you can by what you say (or what you tell yourself).

As with the first step, this requires a degree of introspection. When you perform certain actions or act in a way that is uncharacteristic, you should take a step back and think about the kind of emotions that typically galvanize such reactions.

For example, if I was somewhat cold and unresponsive to my friend, I would need to think about what happened between us that subconsciously annoyed me. It might stem back to something as small as him never having his wallet when the bill comes.

Notice how you act when you experience certain emotions, and you'll begin to see certain patterns emerging.

At this point, it's very easy to slip into judgment mode and start attaching labels to your behavior. If you are acting in a way you shouldn't be acting, it's easy to judge yourself as a loser or a bad person.

This would be a mistake that will just lead to a slippery slope of negativity. Your main focus right now is simply to get a clear picture. It's very hard to come up with an honest picture if you're constantly judging yourself.

Once you have that, you can work on the following step.

The third step is to practice responding instead of reacting.

People with high emotional intelligence eventually come to the realization that they can control their emotional states. This is made possible by knowing the causes and addressing them at that moment.

It's not so much of a confrontation with other people; it's the self-talk that is "That's why I was upset. It's not actually a big deal. I should have no problem going back to my normal mood now."

That's the meaning of responding versus reacting. Letting your emotions govern you means you are reacting instead of responding.

Responding is crucial because it involves premeditation. You're taking all the factors into consideration and making an informed choice as to what to say and how to act. Reaction, on the other hand, is simply letting your emotions get the best of you. It's often unbalanced and in many cases, leads to a downward spiral of negative reactions.

For example, when you react negatively to somebody it provokes a negative response in turn, and you then respond even more negatively. It's a race to the bottom.

Put a label and cause on your emotion so you can bring yourself back to your status quo.

Knowing yourself must come first. Analyze yourself and

base your empathy from this level of self-analysis. If you're not self-aware, all your efforts at trying not to step on people's toes will fail. They will ultimately become self-serving. Your inability to get around your emotions will tint your reading of how other people feel.

Here's a short list of factors you need to focus on to boost your emotional intelligence. It's not an easy task because you can't focus on one factor definitively. You must be adaptable in discovering why people feel what they currently do.

How your thoughts and actions affect others and how they might be misinterpreted.

What are other people's primary motivations and what unspoken, underlying motivations might they have that they are not even aware of?

Consider people's built-in biases and life circumstances that give rise to certain emotions.

How people display their emotions both positively and negatively.

How do they display these in different ways?

What is the range of expression that people normally use?

By being aware of these factors, you increase your emotional intelligence because you are able to read people more accurately. And just as important, you can respond to them in a more calibrated manner that leads to fewer negative reactions.

A final way you can increase your emotional intelligence is what I mentioned earlier in Chapter 3: read fiction.

This is how you can practice empathy in an infinite number of situations. Even in a short story, there are clear motivations and reasons that people act a certain way to drive the plot. It's worth, at least once, doing the exercise of writing out all the characters, their character history, and exactly why they are acting as they do in the story. Then, come up with two more reasons why they are acting a certain way – because you never know. Having these alternative possibilities in mind cultivates emotional intelligence in a way that lets you into other people's heads.

At the most basic level, emotional intelligence is knowing the relatively objective set of reactions to any given statement or circumstance, and the difference between the various subjective reactions.

For example, if you insult someone's mother in a serious manner with a serious face, the relatively objective reaction would be anger and being offended. You can expect that reaction a majority of the time. However, what are the other possible reactions, and what accounts for the difference? People might assume you are joking, laugh out of confusion, or ignore you because they didn't even hear what you said.

Emotional intelligence will allow you to connect with people on a deeper level because you understand them implicitly without their saying anything. You will just get them. This is what many people interpret as chemistry and rapport, and you will have it in a seemingly effortless manner.

Chapter 8. Agreeable Boundaries

Generally speaking, we all want to be agreeable and not difficult.

We want people to see us positively because they know we are pleasant and agreeable in all sorts of situations. Isn't being agreeable the hallmark of a good team player at work, and a fun friend to be around?

Let's examine how most people define being agreeable.

Being accommodating. Being adaptable. Being flexible. Perhaps above all else, letting other people have their way.

Generally speaking, this can be a good thing. Who doesn't want to be agreeable? But the problem is there are, and should be, limits to this strategy.

There is a big difference between getting along with somebody and becoming a doormat with no boundaries. You don't want to be taken advantage of, and at times it can be difficult to draw the line.

Unfortunately, many people who try to be agreeable fall into this exact trap. They blur the line for themselves and all of a sudden, instead mutually beneficial situations, they end up serving other people's self-interests and ignoring their own.

Instead of being viewed in a positive light, they are viewed as gullible or weak-willed. You might think you're getting along well with these people, but in reality, they might be thinking you are two-faced or have no set of principles you would gladly fight for.

The bottom line is being completely agreeable can also be unhealthy and can lead to your enabling negative behaviors on both sides. If you try to be too nice and let people do what they want, you will become a doormat. This is bad for your self-esteem as well as for your social perception.

You need to be able to set boundaries to make sure this doesn't happen. You have to resolve to be looked at by other people as a person with your own agency and your own core principles. You can't simply allow yourself to be dismissed as a part of a mindless group of people that can easily be deceived, manipulated, or stepped on.

At work, it's probably better to fall on the more agreeable side. In a business setting, with proven sharks, it's probably better to fall on the side of more boundaries.

So how do you navigate the balance between agreeableness and boundaries to form... *agreeable boundaries*?

First, what are boundaries?

Objectively, they are limits where you are not being taken advantage of in an unfair manner. Subjectively, they are limits to what you're willing to do or accommodate. To most, this is where we start to feel as if we're being used or manipulated.

How do you have good boundaries but also remain agreeable and flexible at the same time? How do you maintain being agreeable while at the same time being assertive as to your needs?

People tend to fall on one side or the other, so the best approach is to determine where you fall on the agreeableness-boundaries spectrum and work toward the middle.

Here's how to know if you need more boundaries:

- You fear awkwardness more than not having your way on something that's important to you.
- You avoid all conflict, even questions that are posed out of curiosity and are not requests.
- You constantly put other people's needs in front of your own.
- You always give people the benefit of the doubt.
- You don't like defending yourself or your choices against any type of criticism.
- You feel threatened and insecure when challenged.
- You are easily convinced or manipulated.

- You accept people's criticism immediately and without question.
- You accommodate out of insecurity and fear of rejection.

Do any of those sound familiar? Then you need to realize that people won't reject you or hate you just because you refuse what they want. If they lack the ability to separate the two, the fault is on them and they are acting out of turn, not you.

You also have to separate yourself from a conflict about a situation, and people's feelings and emotions towards you. They likely won't change over small issues – really, any issue that isn't offensive or insulting won't change their feelings toward you.

If you feel like someone will lose their respect for you because of a simple disagreement, or someone might be upset at not getting their way for once – you need more boundaries.

It comes down to breaking the assumptions of negativity that come along with a disagreement. We avoid these feelings for years, and it seems so simple to just let other people have their way. Sometimes it might be, but there is a cumulative effect that is enabling behavior on the part of both parties.

Remember that there is an objective and subjective component to the agreeableness-boundary line. Just make sure you aren't compromising everything in a subjective manner.

On the flip side, here's how to know if you need to be more agreeable:

- You see things in black or white.
- You think things like "My way or the highway."
- You are unwilling to accommodate based on principle.
- You ignore other people's needs.
- You view your needs as more important.
- You feel that things will fall apart if you don't get your way.
- You don't recognize a difference between your way and the right way.
- You have rigid and arbitrary yes/no rules.
- You nitpick about details that don't matter.
- You are quickly dismissive of others.
- You feel the need to assert your opinion.
- You feel huge insecurity about being incorrect.

This is when you need to loosen up a little bit and start to bend with the wind more. In some rare occasions in the office, matters might truly be black and white. But especially in social situations, you need to bend if you want any semblance of charm or likability.

Very quickly, people will figure out that you only want your way, and that's the highway to nowhere. Nowhere being a location where people don't want to spend time with you, and don't want to even speak to you.

People will respect you more if you are adaptable and not stuck in one mode of thinking. People don't generally like stubborn people. On the other hand, you don't want to be a doormat. Putting up too many boundaries will make you look selfish and rigid. On the other hand, if you are too agreeable, you open the way to being consistently taken advantage of.

Where does the balance truly lie? The answer is different for everyone.

For example, what if I truly enjoy helping a friend move, where others might despise the idea of physical labor for which they aren't getting paid?

Most people fall more on one side of the spectrum, and have a large degree of flexibility.

The next steps are to try to take notice of how you approach situations where there isn't unanimous agreement. What is your natural inclination, and are you acting out of any of the bullet points above?

Examine each situation from the objective measure of fairness. After that, think about whether you're acting out of your own accord or simply reacting to the relationship dynamic.

Chapter 9. Open the door! Belief Police!

Have you ever had that feeling that you just needed to set the record straight on something?

It might not even concern you, and it certainly doesn't affect your life. The other person also likely won't care that much.

In cases like this, if you were to really think about it, it becomes fairly clear that we are only doing this for ourselves.

Why, exactly?

Because you can't stand the idea of someone believing something that you don't. In short, you are a member of the Belief Police.

This causes us to spend way too much time squabbling over things that really don't move the needle just because we feel that other people believe or think something different than we do and must be corrected.

If you've ever been around a know-it-all, you know exactly what I'm talking about. If you don't, you might be a badge-carrying member of the Belief Police.

Whomever you're speaking with, there will inevitably come a point where you don't match up with them.

If it's about a topic that you have a personal investment in, it's easy to get in over your head and try to win the other person to your side. You think, "How could anyone think any differently? The conclusion is so clear!"

But how often does it actually matter beyond that very minute that you're thinking about it?

The vast majority of the time, this kind of squabbling occurs in places like the comments section of a YouTube video or the comments section of a news blog. When you scroll down into the rabbit hole, you will see people arguing over the smallest pedantry and nitpicking for days. Mostly, the arguments are between two people who simply don't want to give any ground.

We feel that since we know so much better than the other person, we have some sort of responsibility to correct them. In other cases, we know that we're right about something and the other person is wrong in a black and white sense. We then take it upon ourselves to prove to them just how smart we are. We just can't stand someone believing something wrong or contrary to what we believe!

These tendencies play out all the time, and in many cases they involve issues that are of very little importance. You want to be right all the time – the Belief Police typically do.

A Belief Policeman might be very effective at imposing their beliefs on others... but this habit is going to make you downright obnoxious to talk to, and not in an affectionately obnoxious kid sister kind of way. People will avoid you. Who wants to spend time with someone who makes them feel judged, attacked, and defensive?

The bottom line is that the bulk of these arguments all stem from the all too human tendency to "police" other people's beliefs.

The underlying assumption is, "I have to show them I'm right and make them bow to my knowledge." Everything is a pissing match – and as is always the case – borne out of supreme insecurity.

Everything is an opportunity to show just how vastly superior your knowledge and experience are compared to the person you are conversing with. Because otherwise, you'd be seen as inadequate and inferior, right? Instead of saying, "Well, you could be right. You might have a point. Moving on!" you stand your ground and want to show intellectual dominance. The great part about this type of statement is you're not making an actual assertion or conceding to their position, you're just validating them and moving on.

Yet...

You have to catch yourself when you slip into this mode because it is not only subtle, but also very addictive because of the payoff at the end. Let's face it, it feels amazing when someone acquiesces and says "Yeah...you're right, I'm wrong."

But at what cost does this come?

And in the end, does it really matter?

If you took an aerial view of your heated conversations with your friends, co-workers, associates, and colleagues, in almost all cases you would probably conclude that almost none of it truly mattered. Your pride and ego did, but not the issue at hand.

Most of the time, the reason you have such arguments is that you have taken on the role of Belief Policeman. You've given yourself the job of patrolling other people's minds, assumptions, and beliefs.

Not only is it completely unnecessary, it is almost always unwelcome.

What if you expressed your religious beliefs and someone couldn't stop trying to convert you to a different religion?

What if you expressed your love of a certain food or drink and someone just couldn't stop telling you how disgusting they were?

What if you expressed your opinion on a favorite movie or

television show and someone couldn't stop telling you that you *needed* to watch other shows?

It's frustrating being the recipient of this attitude because you feel attacked, and it's not as if they are going to change your mind anyway. It's futile. So what gives you reason to think that it's not going to be unwelcome when you do it to other people?

It says more about you than it does about them if you feel the need to constantly interject your opinions and thoughts. Being part of The Belief Police is for your benefit, not theirs, even though in your mind you are seeking to benefit them with your knowledge.

You're just stroking your ego.

Follow this simple rule to break out of this behavior pattern: don't share your opinion unless asked.

Keep it simple. Unless someone has asked you for your opinion, or is quite obviously soliciting your arguments as part of a debate, don't engage them.

Err on the side of neutral.

Engage momentarily just to acknowledge that they do have an opinion and you might even throw in your opinion there, but don't attempt to convince or police them.

This is especially true when it comes to matters of taste and opinion. These are completely subjective. What looks good to you might be completely ugly to another person. You won't convince anyone to like chocolate more than they already do, or to like beets when they hate them, so, it's really a waste of your time — and an extremely annoying one at that — to exert your energy trying to convince them.

The bottom line: if something is not affecting you directly, or it's a one-time occurrence and the issue is something that is near and dear to your heart, choose to resist the temptation to be the Belief Police. In fact, resist the temptation more than that.

Just let others be right (or think they are right) most of the time. Choose your battles and don't fret about the small details of what you can't change. You'll be happier and less stressed, and you'll notice a direct correlation between that and the quality of your friendships and interactions.

Chapter 10. The Four Communication Styles

When I was still practicing law, it was no surprise that I would often come across aggressive personalities.

These were the types of people that wanted to dominate their opponents, whether in the courtroom, through documents, or in the cafeteria. They went to law school to try to be the best, and their goal-orientedness was occasionally admirable.

However, they are a large part of the reason I got out of the legal industry. I had a sense of dread when I would open emails from opposing counsel, and occasionally from my supervising partners.

Meetings were never very pleasant, and I found myself often thinking "Hey, why can't we all just relax a little bit?"

The reality was that I didn't know there were different communication styles, and what drove the people that adhere to each style.

I could get along just fine with people that were relaxed – in other words, similar to me. But that wasn't going to help me very much when dealing with strangers and generally getting where I wanted to be.

One of the many keys to playing well with others, no matter who they are, is being able to identify their communication style and thus understand them better.

This is about understanding how they're different from you and understanding how these differences can be reflected in the ways they choose to communicate what they believe and what they think.

By using this style-based approach to friends and strangers, you can create a framework with which to deal with people – and it might surprise you in how well it works. We can come up with a semi-predictable map on how to deal with certain types of people.

By the same token, by knowing how certain personality types tend to think, behave, and interact socially, we can also avoid unnecessary conflict and awkward moments.

For example, if I knew there were four main communication styles and that I was dealing with aggressive communication, I would know to speak in a way that furthered their goals and to avoid pleasantries and small talk. The currency of an aggressive communicator is often progress toward goals. And that's how you can become likable with someone like that.

There are four main communication styles – attempt to discover which most describes you, and which most fits the people you spend the most time with. The four styles are: Passive, Aggressive, Passive-Aggressive, and Assertive.

Knowing someone's style can transform how you interact with them. Sometimes, it can be like a lightning bolt of clarity, not unlike when you stare at a pattern and suddenly the three-dimensional picture starts to form in your head out of the pattern.

Passive Communication

Passive communicators avoid expressing their opinions or feelings.

They avoid any type of conflict, and this involves standing their ground and even claiming their rightful privilege. None of that matters to them; they'd prefer that others draw attention to them instead of doing it themselves.

They often see their needs ignored.

Passive communicators tend to speak softly or apologetically. When passive people talk, they usually convey one of the following feelings:

- I won't stand up for myself or my rights.
- I don't know what my rights are, and I don't care.
- I am okay being a doormat.
- I need the help of others to assert myself.
- No one, including me, considers my feelings.

You can see the common thread – passive communicators don't feel secure in their abilities or identity, and this fear keeps them silent and out of the spotlight. The best way to engage passive communicators is to approach them gently, make sure you don't use judgmental language, and encourage them by complimenting and emphasizing their worth.

They'll be reserved and guarded until they feel safe with you.

Yes, you might feel like you need to coddle the passive communicator. It is low self-esteem that has left them interpersonally crippled.

Aggressive Communication

Aggressive communicators tend to be self-centered. It's not intentional, but they think more about themselves and thus tend to violate the space of others.

It's not just confidence, but over-confidence because it goes beyond personal boundaries and is driven by a need to dominate, conquer, and prove others wrong.

People with an aggressive communication style are always out to prove a point. It is not uncommon for aggressive communicators to be verbally or physically abusive, or both. You would be right in expecting that they also react poorly when challenged or proved wrong.

Aggressive communication is typically the result of low self-esteem.

Many people who have an aggressive communication style are suffering from unhealed emotional wounds and deep down feel powerless. Aggressive individuals display a low tolerance for frustration and tend to use humiliation and conversation interruption to try to assert themselves. In their minds, they're simply standing up for their rights, because they've made the mistake of not standing up for them before.

In a sense, it's the mindset of "I'll never be disrespected again," but objectively speaking they're disrespecting other people.

Accordingly, they'll use whatever is available to them to stand up, often involving criticism or blaming or attacking others.

They tend to be goal-oriented around this, so they have a tendency not to be good listeners.

Aggressive communicators express statements that convey the following:

- The other person is inferior and wrong.
- The problem is all the other person's fault.
- I am superior and correct as a rule.
- I'm going to get my way regardless of the negative consequences.
- I am entitled to things and other people owe me.

Aggressive communicators are often uncomfortable with themselves, and they lash out at other people to alleviate that tension and make themselves feel better. A direct challenge to an aggressive communicator can escalate quickly into a pissing match where there will never be a winner.

Knowing that they are focused on protecting their perceived rights and getting what they feel is owed them, you should handle aggressive communicators as you would an angry child.

Validate them and let them know they have been heard. Placation, in other words, is the action prescription. Once they can see that you recognize their greatness, or are simply not a threat to their pride and ego, they will let you in.

It might seem as if they've created a club for the people that are acceptable to them, and sometimes it pays to be in that club.

Passive-Aggressive Communication

Passive-aggressive communicators appear passive on the surface.

And of course, deep down, they are acting passively with a purpose, and out of anger.

They are like ducks – serene on the surface, but paddling furiously just below the water line.

Passive-aggressive communicators use subtlety, misdirection, and contrived tests to communicate their message and attempt to get their way.

They want to assert dominance over people and a situation, but they want to do it in a way that lets them appear socially acceptable and polite. Confrontation is their worst nightmare.

Passive-aggressive communication usually has an undercurrent of powerlessness and resentment. They want to scream at someone, but lack the courage and social awareness to do so. Therefore, their alienation and bitterness grows, and eventually, they feel incapable of dealing directly with the object of their irritation, frustration, and resentment.

They always try to do things in a roundabout way because they cannot handle direct confrontation. They feel weak in such situations, which is why they always look for subtle ways to deliver what otherwise would be an attack.

They express their anger by subtly undermining the real or imagined object or person they resent. They mutter to themselves instead of confronting another person. They smile at you even though they're angry. They speak with sarcasm, double meanings, and veiled threats.

When passive-aggressive individuals communicate, they convey the following messages:

- I feel insecure with confrontation so I sabotage and disrupt.
- Why can't they understand what I'm feeling?
- I will appear cooperative on the outside, but I secretly

hope for your failure.

- I'm really angry, but I can't show it.
- You're stupid for not seeing my passive-aggressive hints and signs.
- I want to get my way, but I won't tell you what it is or how to get it. Figure it out.

Unlike the other two communicators, passive-aggressive communicators aren't driven solely by insecurity. They are driven by a combination of insecurity and deep bitterness about being overlooked by others. They feel they deserve better, but don't know how to express it.

Therefore, the way to deal with passive-aggressive communicators is to validate their feelings. Make it known that you've noticed their signs, even if you haven't and need to fabricate something to acknowledge, and ask them to clarify what you've missed and exactly what they want.

This way, they can feel that their underhanded tactics and maneuvers actually worked. This gives them exactly what they want – control and dominance over a situation without having to resort to confrontation.

Assertive Communication

This last communication style happens to be the ideal approach.

Assertive communicators clearly state their opinions and feelings and firmly advocate for their rights and needs.

What makes this different from aggressive communication

is that there is no need to violate the rights of others. You objectively recognize what your rights are, and where the boundaries lie, and assert them as a matter of fact. You don't need to step on others to get yours.

Assertive communication is a result of high and healthy self-esteem.

Assertive people value themselves, their time, their emotional, spiritual, and physical needs. These types of people have chosen to be strong advocates for themselves while being respectful of the rights of others. They don't believe that for them to win, other people have to lose.

On the other hand, they have no reservations about standing up for themselves and aren't uncomfortable with conflict when dealing with any of the other communication styles.

Assertive people feel connected with others and they state their needs and feelings clearly, appropriately, and respectfully. They are in control of their emotions and speak in calm and clear tones. They are good listeners, maintain good eye contact, and create a respectful environment for others. They do not allow others to abuse or manipulate them.

When assertive people communicate with others, they convey the following messages:

- I am confident in who I am.
- I will make the best of this situation.
- I speak honestly and directly without ulterior motives.

- I know what I deserve and don't accept anything less.
- I have faults and admit them freely.
- I have boundaries and will not tolerate certain behavior.

How do you deal with assertive communicators? Well, hope that everyone you come across is one, because they are the easiest to speak to. There is no best practice because they are adaptable and can deal expertly with any communication style.

That's why this is the style to aspire to. They speak honestly and you don't get the sense that they're trying to accomplish something involving you behind your back.

Notably, they are not driven by the need to prove themselves or protect their self-perception. It's amazing what self-esteem can do, and shows that if you are comfortable with yourself, others will be as well. It's the internal struggle of not feeling good enough and attempting to compensate that drives the negative aspects of other communication styles.

I would love to say that just by having identified these four styles, that I can firmly put myself into the assertive category. But that's not always true, and it won't be true for you either.

And that's okay. We're all human, and no matter where on the spectrum you fall, (1) knowing that there is indeed a difference, and (2) having a framework to understand their motivations and how to deal with them will help you immensely with people, inside and out of work.

Chapter 11. The Masters

Enough from me.

In the quest to become a better people person and increase interpersonal skills, it's helpful to look at common themes from true masters on the subject. These are household names and I've isolated and analyzed some of their approaches and mindsets regarding interpersonal skills.

You'll notice some common threads on how to be better with others and work through any tough situation.

Consider that these titans made it to the top of their fields not because of their inherent skills, but because of how they are able to work with, and against, people.

"Two monologues do not make a dialogue." - Jeff Daly

Jeff Daly is a prominent American architect who previously served as head of design of the Metropolitan Museum of Art in New York.

What is this quote saying?

First, when you speak with someone, you must make sure that it's a two-way street. It's not a lecture, and it's not sermon. It's an interactive dialogue where two parties collaborate to create something together.

Second, when you speak with someone, make sure that you are actually listening and engaged, as opposed to ceding the floor and simply waiting for your turn to speak again without acknowledging them.

Conversations are best viewed as opportunities for learning. They can be opportunities for building bridges instead of each party attempting to show just how intelligent they are.

For real dialogues to take place, you have to have an open mind regarding what you can take away from the other person as far as your own personal education is concerned.

Keep an open mind, develop a sense of curiosity, and most important, attempt to be less self-centered – this is how you create meaningful and healthy dialogues.

"You can make more friends in two months by becoming interested in other people than you can in two years by trying to get other people interested in you." - *Dale Carnegie*

Dale Carnegie was the author of the seminal book, *How to Win Friends and Influence People*. He was widely regarded as a pioneer of the self-development movement, and his legacy continues today. There's a reason many people call his works generic and common sense – he's the one who made them so.

What exactly does Carnegie mean here?

It's not very easy to make friends if you're constantly trying to impress other people and paint a good picture of yourself for them. In fact, that's downright counterproductive to making friends. All you're doing is becoming the windbag that lacks self-awareness and whom no one is interested in.

Instead, taking an interest in people and letting them speak and share about themselves is how people are more inclined to make friends.

We like people who are interested in us and think we are amazing. We also enjoy speaking about ourselves – most people are their own favorite topic and we like to explain our unique sensibilities. Seize advantage of this very simple fact and become more interested and curious about others and give them an outlet. You'll find that if you barely speak during a conversation, the other person will walk away feeling as if they've had an amazing experience.

Showing intense interest is an everyday superpower that will open people up more than you might expect.

"Many attempts to communicate are nullified by saying too much." - Robert Greenleaf

Robert Greenleaf was the founder of the Servant Leadership movement, which is a leadership philosophy and approach toward managing people.

At this point, one of the common themes should be showing itself fairly obviously.

Setting aside what you want in a conversation can be key to having a good one. In other words, focusing on the other person and what they want out of the interaction, and what they want to say will lead to better communication.

You listen, hear concerns, allow them to speak, and validate them. That's difficult if you monopolize communication and only talk about your interests. Not only does nothing get accomplished, but if it does, it doesn't get done well because you didn't receive any feedback from others.

Communication's all about give and take. If you hog the spotlight, you run the risk of being not only a boring communicator, but an annoying one.

Take an opposite tactic. Try to say as little as possible and get other people to speak more.

"I don't like that man. I must get to know him better." - Abraham Lincoln

Abraham Lincoln was the 16th President of the United States of America and is famous for delivering the Gettysburg Address, abolishing slavery, presiding over the presidency during the Civil War, and ultimately being assassinated.

Lincoln hit the nail on the head here.

The reason we don't like people or some people tend to irritate us is because we simply don't know them all that well. What little we do know we take and magnify and amplify, creating a caricatured version of them in our heads that is in no way accurate to real life.

We take what we see in the first 30 seconds from someone and if it's negative, we assume that's their character. We have no reason to give them the benefit of the doubt. We judge.

But everybody bleeds, they hurt, and everybody, deep down, has the same basic wants and needs.

Somebody might come off as obnoxious to you, but if you give them the opportunity to create a three-dimensional identity for themselves, you might find aspects of them that you actually enjoy or admire. Or at least defensible justification for why they are the way they are.

You won't merely label them as obnoxious – they still might be, but they'll be a good person that is occasionally obnoxious, as opposed to unquestioned vermin.

In many cases, people are not inherently bad or good. Our impressions are usually just reflections of our assumptions or attitudes. Give people the benefit of the doubt and talk to them with an open mind.

"Everything that irritates us about others can lead us to an understanding of ourselves." - Carl Jung

Carl Jung was one of the most influential psychologists in

modern history, to be mentioned in the same sentence as Freud and Maslow. He is best known for his work on what are now called Jungian archetypes and the work that eventually became the Myers-Briggs Personality Test.

This quote says volumes about external perception.

As the old saying goes, "When you point a finger, there are three fingers pointing back at you." In almost all cases, the things that really annoy us about other people are really subconscious issues that we, ourselves, share.

This is a deep and profound truth because if we simply allow ourselves to step into the shoes of other people in our conversations with them, we start looking at others as mirrors. Instead of dismissing people as cartoons or exaggerations of our biases and fears, we start seeing ourselves in others. It can be the most liberating realization in the world.

It also encourages us to observe and listen more. If we closely observe what we judge in others, we can learn volumes about ourselves.

"Wise men speak because they have something to say; fools, because they have to say something." - Plato

Plato was one of the most prominent Ancient Greek philosophers, along with his teacher Socrates and his student Aristotle.

This is another remark on the importance of listening.

Wise people spend their time listening, observing, and thinking about the matters before them. Consequently, when they speak, people listen, because what they have to say is usually measured and wise. They think twice as much as they speak because that's the best way to become wiser.

Fools on the other hand spend their time not increasing their knowledge by speaking, interjecting, and interrupting. This is the best way to not understand people and appear uninformed at the same time.

Communication is best when informed and measured, and silence is not always a bad thing.

When you are going to speak, try asking yourself the reason for it.

Is it because you have something to contribute, or you just want to fill the air or hear your own voice? What is necessary to say, and what should be discarded in favor of hearing the other person?

What common themes did you pick up in the quotes above?

- It's more important to listen than be heard.
- Communication is not about speaking.
- Self-understanding helps you relate to people and listening is an important part of this process.
- Empathy is created by humanizing others.
- Curiosity and interest are essentially communication aphrodisiacs.
- Learning and allowing others to teach you is not self-centered.

Chapter 12. Empathy Matters

Empathy is the ability to accurately put yourself in someone else's shoes and experience what they are feeling.

It's rare because most people either don't care enough, or can only humor others in a superficial manner.

If you can't bother with empathy, it's like not knowing the difference in how to treat someone who's just come from a funeral, and someone who just attended a wedding.
Most of the time, of course, it's much subtler than that.
How do you know how to interpret someone's sudden change in vocal tone, or the way that they closed the door? How do you know if someone is enjoying your company or not? How do you know if someone is really laughing at your jokes or just being polite?

How can you truly get inside someone's head to understand how they are feeling?

Being a people person is about innately understanding as

many perspectives as possible.

Take Patricia Moore, for example. She is a prime example of taking the extra step to understand others and thus be able to speak for them.

Moore was an American designer who conducted an experiment in the 1970s that fundamentally changed people's notions about empathy.

What began as a social experiment quickly turned into something more. She, at the age of 26, dressed up as an 85-year old woman to investigate what life was like for an elderly person. Specifically – what were the challenges they faced as a result of old age, and how could those challenges be conquered?

On and off for three full years, Moore donned full makeup, walked with a limp to simulate arthritis, and wrapped herself in bandages to fake ailments and illnesses. To complete her transformation into an elderly person, she wore thick glasses that she couldn't see well out of. The illusion was complete.

In this guise, she visited many cities and acted as an elderly woman might. She rode public transportation, navigated stores, and generally tried her hand at everyday life, essentially handicapped by her advanced age and various ailments.

Based on her experiences, she walked away with a profoundly new perspective on product design. It turned out that designs in America are focused predominantly on people who are younger and more able.

Can openers, doors, and other modern amenities were bundled up with all sorts of assumptions regarding physical ability. These products were designed for those who are in the prime of their lives. They are not very friendly to children and they were definitely outright hostile to the physical limitations of elderly Americans. They were not very accommodating or convenient for those with simple ailments such as weak hands or poor eyesight.

Based on these experiences and her difficulties, she came up with new product designs that can be used by elderly people. For example, instead of regular potato peelers with thin handles, she padded these with thick rubber to enable older people with reduced grips to use them comfortably.

She also invented new kitchen products that can easily be used by people suffering from arthritis. Based on her three-year experience, she became one of the most outspoken and prominent elderly rights advocates in the United States. Thanks, in large part, to her own personal efforts at understanding modern life from the perspective of an older American, the Americans with Disabilities Act (ADA) was passed.

Her latest project is designing rehabilitation centers for U.S. war veterans with missing limbs or brain injuries so they can relearn to live independently, doing everything from buying groceries to using a cash machine.

What can be learned from Patricia Moore's experience?

By simply choosing to walk a mile in another person's shoes, we begin to see the world in a very different way. We also begin to detect our unconscious biases. Take a regular can opener, most people would not think twice about using a can opener with a thin handle, but if you were an older person with arthritis and mobility issues, it can be quite a challenge. Patricia Moore broke through these personal barriers that are often unspoken and invisible by assuming the physical limitations of another person.

Her experience is a very powerful testimony to how well we can improve ourselves and the world around us by simply choosing to be open-minded and actively seeking to look at the world through the eyes of people we, at least on the surface, don't have much in common with. You have to seek out ways you can play out Patricia Moore's experiment in your life.

For example, what are the struggles that your friends or coworkers are going through? Suppose one of them is going through a divorce. It's worth visualizing the struggles in that, and even doing some research so you understand them better. There are certain triggers and anxieties associated with divorce, not to mention created by it, and you would relate to them exponentially better if you just engaged in this thought exercise from time to time.

Seek out ways you can do this in your life with the people around you. What about them don't you understand or are completely ignorant about? Remedy your ignorance. Understanding means that you're not just guessing or winging it – it means that you can succeed with people in whatever way you wish.

Talk to people and try to detect the assumptions they hold. Ask them questions that can relate to past experiences that might explain why they believe what they believe. While these opinions may normally be annoying, offensive, or ridiculous to you, the more you look at things from their perspective, the more things will make sense to you. Not only will you become a better conversationalist, you'll become a better person to be around.

By simply choosing to be more selfless and curious about others' perspectives, you will actually start to understand people. There's a big difference between understanding others and simply guessing. When you guess, you're still stuck with your own personal biases and stereotypes. Understanding can only come from actually experiencing or viewing things from another person's truly distinct perspective.

Chapter 13. Workplace Tactics

As important as you might assume interpersonal skills and people tactics are in your personal life, they can make or break you at the office and sabotage your livelihood.

In our social and personal lives, we generally choose people that we like and enjoy being around. It's no accident who we spend time with, and we simply avoid those we don't have anything in common with.

Of course, this is the opposite of a working environment. The only thing you might have in common with your cubicle mate might be the fact that you both applied to the same company at around the same time. These people might be fundamentally different than you, but your career trajectory is greatly impacted by how well you get along with them.

To make things even more difficult, the workplace is fraught with situations that are tense, confrontational, or just plain uncomfortable. It's what happens in an environment where people are objectively evaluated on performance under a clear hierarchy.

Telling a coworker that he smells? Sitting someone down and letting them know that their work just isn't up to snuff?

God forbid, firing someone?

It doesn't matter how smart or how well intentioned you are, no one excels in the office in a vacuum. Beyond being likable and a pleasant person to be around, you need to know how to handle the uncomfortable situations that will inevitably arise.

If you put in 100 points of effort toward interpersonal skills for social situations, you should put in 500 points in the workplace.

There are a few main tactics you must learn to employ in the office for better likability and workplace cachet.

Conflict Management

Even if you're not a manager or a supervisor, you need this ability.

Regardless of your label or title, it thrusts you into the leader position organically. People will begin to rally around you when they have problems of any sort, and you just may become the "go-to" person when personal conflicts arise.

It's only a matter of time until your supervisors and managers recognize this and you get promoted.

What is the best way to manage conflict?

Look at the arguments of each side and try to name three things that they each want. Instead of competing over the one objective, they now have three ways for them to gain a happy resolution from the conflict.

For example, often people just want validation, credit, or recognition. This is something we take for granted that motivates others. What if you discovered someone was truly looking for that as opposed to the same promotion as you?

Use your creativity, intelligence, and the information you know about the parties involved to craft win-win resolutions instead of naming a black-or-white loser. This is not going to happen unless you effectively respect differences of opinions.

Problem-Solving

If you reduce it down, every single business exists to solve a problem. They provide an answer or service that makes a problem easier to deal with, or eliminates it entirely.

If you're hungry, a grocery store helps you reduce your hunger. If you break your foot, a doctor solves the problem of your pain and health.

With problem-solving in the workplace, the focus should be on taking the best course of action while simultaneously accounting for the needs and desires of others.

If there is not a way to do it simultaneously, this is something you must actively think about balancing. What will get your desired outcome but not make your coworkers jealous, your boss think you are sucking up, and give others a poor impression of you?

For example, there's a negative way to solve problems – interrupt other people, not credit others, hog the spotlight, overly praise yourself, and not include others. And there's a way that will account for others – include others, praise them, collaborate, validate their concerns, and generally make them feel invested.

What you're really cultivating is your sense of thoughtfulness and considerateness.

And by being the most thoughtful person in the bunch, you will be the one people trust with their issues and concerns, even if you aren't responsible for them.

Communication

In the workplace, there are countless shenanigans as far as power plays and personality clashes go.

In almost all cases, communication is the first thing to suffer. By resolving to speak clearly and directly while being sensitive to the people you're speaking with, you can establish yourself as a great communicator.

A lot of people take a lot of pains to avoid uncomfortable conversations. These people are driven by fear and become passive-aggressive. They know they'd rather deal with the situation, but they feel stuck.

Ultimately, instead of making the problem go away by dealing with it directly and working with people respectfully, they end up being perceived as backstabbers. Don't let this happen to you.

For example, if you hated how someone formatted their pages because it caused you an extra hour of work, is there a way to frame that problem about the extra work versus their incompetency with word processing?

Frame issues on the consequences, not their actions. Focus on the facts and never implications.   Question your assumptions and give others the benefit of the doubt.

Listening

Listening in the workplace is especially important because people are constantly evaluated by their abilities and shortcomings.

You must be able to listen to people's perspectives and issues without judging them. Make them feel safe opening up to you and being vulnerable.

This sounds easy, but you might be terribly dismissive in ways you don't realize. A simple eye-roll, a scoff, an eyebrow raise, a palm slammed into a forehead, or a judging tone could spell your doom.

You have to allow yourself not only to fully open your ears to what they have to say, but open your mind as well – and then show it to them physically. Keep an inquisitive face and make sure to ask questions with a tone of genuine curiosity. People are fine with the sizzle of the spotlight if they don't feel there will be a negative backlash.

Internally, think through their thought processes. Look at their assumptions. Try to piece things together and come up with their perspective. Why did they arrive at the conclusion that they have?

For example, if a coworker comes to you and confides that they feel inadequate and that they are terrible at their marketing assignments, don't agree and make fun of them. There are better ways to acknowledge their insecurities and make them feel better about them.

Finally, learn to recognize whether people are actually asking for a solution or just letting off some steam.

Accountability

In any organization, there will always be people who try to make themselves look better by shifting the blame to others.

For example, a new marketing director starts a job and figures out that she is in over her head. So, what does she do? She blames the previous marketing director and paints such a terrible picture that the CEO accepts the new marketing director's dismal results as an improvement.

You're only setting the bar very low for yourself, and guess what? The people who matter will take notice; it's human nature to live up to our lowest expectations. By not pushing yourself to your fullest potential, by choosing to consistently lower your standards, you will eventually write yourself out of any career advances. You're hurting your own work ethic and others' perception of you.

Stop making excuses or blaming others.

Instead, take full responsibility and look at your difficulties as a puzzle and personal challenge to your creativity and imagination. By looking at things as a game to master or a puzzle to solve, you challenge yourself to come up with creative solutions that will not only take your personal performance to the next level, but your company as well.

Appreciation

This can be as simple as saying "Thank you" or "Great job," but it's something that is missing more often than not in our workplace relationships.

Just because it is someone's job to deliver something doesn't mean they won't feel good if you voice appreciation for it and praise them.

You have to let other people know you value them and their help. Just because a person is low on the totem pole doesn't mean they are worthless. Each and every one of them works so that you can focus on what you bring to the table, no matter how high or low-value it is.

Let others know that you appreciate and value their usefulness. By simply being appreciative and being genuine about it, you can go a long way in becoming a source of emotional reassurance in your organization.

For example, if one of your subordinates brings you a report you asked for on a tight deadline, you could take them aside and thank them for working long hours and tell them how much you appreciate the work they put in, and that your work would be impossible without them, and that their superiors will definitely know about their work.

Especially powerful is when you show appreciation and praise in front of other people, coworkers and supervisors alike. It builds a congenial and encouraging workplace culture and creates multiple sources of positivity instead of just you. Finally, it's a driving source of positive conditioning.

Chapter 14. Interpersonal Leadership

In any organization, there are always two types of leaders: formal and organic leaders.

Formal leaders are the people you see on an organizational chart.

They are people who occupy distinct places in an organization's hierarchy. These are managers, supervisors, team leaders, division heads, vice presidents, presidents, and so on down the line. This is formal leadership because you are a leader by appointment.

People will look at you as a leader not because they want to, but because they have to.

You occupy a space in the organizational chart of the firm or establishment. You may not have solid interpersonal skills, you might not even have any, but it doesn't really matter because people are compelled to say you are leader. Of course, such compelled obedience and respect tends to be very shallow. When it comes to crunch time and things that really matter as far as the day to day operations of any organization, the success of any firm or outfit depends on how many organic leaders there are.

When I was in college, I worked a few side jobs for extra money. All the jobs I had after I got my degree followed this pattern. I notice that when I entered the doors, there were always "official" leaders and "organic" leaders.

Organic leaders are people whom coworkers instinctively and naturally flock around. When it comes to forming an opinion or expressing the sentiments of coworkers or collaborating regarding an event or solving an issue, my coworkers always went to the same handful of people.

Looking back after working several corporate jobs, I found certain patterns. These people have different names, they look very different from each other, they come from different walks of life, but they all have certain things in common.

By taking your interpersonal skills to a certain level, leadership will naturally follow. You might not get that shiny name tag that says you're the manger immediately, but it's only a matter of time. Career success, as far as promotions go, will arrive sooner than later if you focus on your organic leadership skills by improving how you handle social situations.

For greater success with people in social and workplace settings, focus on becoming an organic leader first and foremost. Worry about the title later, if at all.

Listen with Intent

Great people persons aren't passive listeners. They participate and are always trying to satisfy a purpose when they listen. They listen with intent.

They don't have a set agenda that they want to hit people over the head with.

Instead, they pay close attention to what people are saying and they try to get to the bottom why people have a certain issue in mind.

Is it something they want to solve? Should someone else be involved? Do they just want to be heard?

If people are all worked up about a certain person or a problem, they ask questions that are not judgmental in nature but reveal why people feel the way they do. They not only give people an opportunity to get stuff off their chest, but they also direct the person's sharing, so that the exchange proceeds more smoothly and intimately.

Two-way Dialogue

An interaction should never be a monologue unless you are on stage and people have paid to come hear you.

What is the purpose of your interaction? It's rarely to dominate the air space and monopolize the speaking. This means you should always seek to create a two-way dialogue.

How can you do this?

First, be sure to ask more questions than you answer. For every response or story you tell, you can seek to ask two questions to keep it balanced.

Second, take an interest in other people and stop being self-centered. There's no way around it – we often create monologues because we're more interested in ourselves than we are in the other person. But suppose that they feel the same way. Wouldn't they want the opportunity to speak?

Third, make it safe for others to share and be vulnerable by suspending judgment.

Help Others Succeed

One of the most interesting experiences I've had is when one of my shift-mates wasn't even an assistant manager. I pointed out that I was very good at noticing scheduling issues.

He then recommended me to our manager as far as scheduling process improvements went. I later found out that he was actually doing this regularly regarding different ideas other people had.

As a result, our unit was the most efficient and productive in the whole company. It was a fairly large company, so people started paying more attention to my shift-mate. It really did not surprise me to learn after several years that this person is now high up in the executive ranks of the company. He did not have a place in the hierarchy, but it was very clear that he cared about the interest of the company as a whole.

He wanted the company to succeed and that's why he took it upon himself to figure out what everybody in his team was good at, and made management aware of what people could contribute. He enabled the team to build on its strengths and take its performance to the next level. He made everybody good around him because he recognized the mutual benefits.

Organic leaders take it upon themselves to make everybody shine around them. They don't shrink away when people express their brilliance. They don't feel threatened when people come up with great ideas. Instead, they look out for the welfare of the team – whether it is a work team, a friend group, or a baseball team. They think of the team as a whole. And by being the glue that holds people together, they rise along with everyone else.

Accepting

Organic leaders are proactive in seeking constructive feedback, even though it may be crouched in negative tones. They don't react emotionally. Instead, they focus on the substance and what they can take from it.

"Constructive" feedback is really a misnomer because most "constructive" feedback is a rebuke or a slam.

But if you are mature enough, you can phrase it in such a

way that it can lead to constructive changes. Organic leaders know all about this. This is why they can pick up positive feedback that is often crouched in negative terms, and rephrase it to heighten the positive tone and pass it on. This then improves the atmosphere or operational processes of an organization.

"God, you are a terrible planner. I hated this weekend!"

It might sting for a second, but why did they have such a poor time? It's a strong reaction that warrants investigation if you can accept the feedback.

By the same token, they proactively address questions and concerns and don't passively wait for them to come to them.

Listening to people and giving them an opportunity to vent their emotions is just an initial part of a larger process.

Organic leaders, on the other hand, proactively step into the shoes of other people and try to see the situation from their end. Once they have a fairly accurate perspective, they try to come up with a win-win situation. This is not always possible, but when it is the results are dramatically superior.

100% Focus

When you have some face time with people, you expect to feel that you matter. You expect that the person will respect you enough to truly listen to you.

Fake hierarchical leaders do this out of obligation and

formality. Because they're just going through the motions, it's very easy for you to feel as if you're falling between the cracks. It's easy for you to walk away with the impression that you don't really matter all that much.

It is no surprise that organic leaders eventually get formal leadership roles, because they make people feel they matter. It's not just the impression that you get. It is the reality. They're sincerely concerned about your issues.

They are sincere in their resolve to help you with your problem. Unfortunately, that's very hard to get when you're dealing with somebody who's just at the meeting because he feels he has to be there.

Don't just go through the motions. Be focused, engaged, and 100% present.

Chapter 15. Handling Negativity

We've all had people in our lives who are emotional black holes.

They'll call you up when they're feeling depressed or upset and unload for hours. They might not even ask how you are, and when they've finished, they'll suddenly be too busy to continue the conversation and give you a chance to talk.

At conversation's end, I feel negative and dragged into an emotional mess, but they feel much lighter and better.

I do want to be there for them, but if I allow myself to be just a sounding board, I eventually start absorbing some of their negativity. It is very corrosive.

There have been many times where I felt genuinely bummed out because my friends were going through such tough times, and I started seeing the world in dark tones.

Thankfully, it dawned on me that in order to help them, I

did not have to assume the same negativity. I could use my interpersonal skills to help redirect that negativity or help make sense of it in such a way that it led to less anger, less depression, and more optimism.

Good people skills can be used to cut tension, relieve depression and despair, and smooth over matters that create or prolong negative emotions and anger.

Instead of passively listening and absorbing their negativity like a sponge, act as mediator.

What do I mean by this?

Be the one that guides them through their misery and helps them discover what truly upsets them. It's true that some people talk through their negativity out loud to others as a catharsis and aren't actually seeking a solution, but that takes a toll on you, especially if it's the same people with the same issues time after time.

This is similar to active listening, where you are using their words and in actuality doing very little except providing an empty canvas for them to fill with their own thoughts.

The first step is to help them realize why they are upset in the first place.

There are the obvious reasons, such as someone being broken up with. But the less obvious and perhaps more important reasons are the ones you'll have to ferret out, such as someone's fear of loneliness or their insecurity. Things may seem obvious to you, but in reality the issue might be caused by something completely unrelated. It might even come right out of left field. This is part intuition and part listening.

Second, most causes of negativity and depression are because of an insecurity of some sort. However, most of us have stalwart defense mechanisms and may never reach this level of radical self-honesty.

Attempt to create a safe space for someone to admit true insecurities. This allows you to address them and really work on them, as opposed to beat around them and work on things they know won't truly make a difference in your negativity.

You can prompt this with leading statements like, "It sounds like you were feeling insecure about X, or like your friends might have been leaving you behind..."

The third step is prompting for solution.

Remember, at this point, we aren't dealing with someone that just wants a listening ear. We're dealing with someone that has a pattern of negativity in their lives that shouldn't continue being placated.

How do you prompt for solution?

Thankfully, it doesn't involve you having to generate idea after idea. The funny part about negativity is most people know deep down inside what needs to be done. They just need to articulate it to themselves and take ownership of it. You can help them along with leading questions such as

"What do you think needs to happen now? Is it something you can do? What about this?"

Try to come away from this conversation with at least one concrete step to put into action. This way, you can occasionally turn negativity into accomplishment and avoid absorbing the negativity.

Mediation doesn't always work because many people just aren't open to it. They aren't ready to hear it, or they don't want to admit any fault or blame. If mediation falls upon deaf ears, try distraction.

In situations where it seems that people are just not going to give an inch, or their tops are about to explode, you have to use your people tactics to distract them and diffuse the situation.

What you're really doing is diverting attention from an issue that has gotten out of hand.

The key here is to distract them long enough, so that the emotional tension subsides sufficiently for you to either have a mature discussion, or forget about it altogether.

It's very hard to use facts and logic when people are reacting emotionally. If people are on the verge of strangling each other, all the facts, logic, and expert arguing in the world are not going to matter all that much.

Once it's gone or sufficiently reduced, you can attempt to turn back into mediation mode. Your main job is not to convince them. Your main job is not to overpower them.

Your main job is to make them feel that you're listening to them to such an extent that they can get rid of the negative atmosphere. Once their emotional equilibrium sets in, you can then start talking about root causes.

On the other hand, sometimes you just need a catharsis.

Sometimes people just need to stick their heads into a pillow and scream.

Catharsis is basically the story that I mentioned in the beginning of this chapter. You just have to allow yourself to become an emotional sounding board to absorb the heat, negativity, anger, or even hate of the person you're trying to calm down.

It's a thankless task because you yourself have to endure some emotional negativity and disturbance. People will throw all sorts of stuff at you just to get issues off their chest. You have to allow them this luxury. You have to give them the time and the space to rant and vent.

The secret to effectively producing a cathartic moment for someone else is to ask pointed questions that will push the other person to let go of all the negativity by expressing it.

Ask questions that lead them to keep putting things on the table, questions that will allow them to make sure that no negative undercurrents remain undisturbed. Your main focus here is to just let the emotions flow. Your job is to allow that person to purge him or herself of all this negative emotions.

Other ways of creating a catharsis are tactics like writing the angriest email you can muster and not sending it. You can burn off your excess negativity verbally and non-verbally – extreme physical activity also helps. The best part about these types of catharsis is that you don't have to be there for it, just encourage it.

Negativity can be like a rock in a stream that you have to flow around like water to shape.

Chapter 16. The Art of Compassion

For a book about people tactics and interpersonal skills, I would be falling short if I didn't talk about compassion.

Throughout, I've attempted to give you some of the concrete, actionable tactics to take in everyday life, but it's just as important to change your basic approach and mindset to others through compassion.

The task is to become a more compassionate person so you can understand others better and feel more in tune with their emotions. You won't find someone that is a people person who is not compassionate.

Compassion is the highest human ideal as far as interpersonal skills go. The problem is, in practical terms, people often have a very selective picture of compassion. We all possess it to some degree, albeit limited.

It's easy to feel bad for and look out for people that matter to you – people in your tight familial and social circle. But human beings occupy many different concentric circles. The farther out the circle people are, the less concerned about them we become.

In some cases, our concern drops off a cliff.

For some people, if somebody falls outside of their family and friend circle, they could not care less. For others, the focus is more on their country, ethnic or religious group, and everybody outside that group doesn't get much consideration. Everybody has different levels of concern as far as how they draw out their level of attachment.

Compassion, in an ideal sense, is your ability to put yourself in other people's shoes regardless of what they look like, regardless of what they believe, regardless of whether they believe in God or not, or which god they believe in, regardless of whether they're male, female, or patriotic.

As long as they're human beings, the ideal vision of compassion is being able to feel other people's pain.

It's important to understand that compassion is not just an abstract ideal that the rest of humanity, and not necessarily you, should subscribe to. That is self-serving. Instead, it should be a trait that you cultivate, practice, and encourage in yourself. Here are some tips for how to develop more compassion.

Visualization

Imagine that a loved one is suffering, something terrible has happened to him or her. Try to imagine the pain they are going through and look at the world through their eyes.

How would it feel?

Imagine yourself in their shoes trying to do things that you normally do, like go to the bathroom, getting up and walking around, picking up the paper— the daily mundanities of normal life that we take for granted.

Can you feel the pain they are going through? Can you feel the uncertainty, the sheer terror, the regret, or the guilt? Try to subject yourself to the barrage of negative emotions that they must be going through.

This may seem exhausting, and it is, but if you practice this for a couple of weeks, you will be better able to imagine the suffering of other people you know.

You'll be surprised how open minded you will become. You will also realize that there's really not much that divides us, and that's an important concept – focusing on similarities of circumstance and emotion.

For example, it's easy for somebody who is earning a lot of money to expect that everybody else should have a certain standard of living and should view the world a certain way. It's easy for us to live in our own bubbles. The same also applies in reverse. If you have always struggled, it's very easy to assume that everybody else is struggling too, and is looking at the world the way you do.

By practicing compassion, you destroy all those artificial

barriers and you truly understand that we all bleed red. We all hunger. We all thirst. We all need love and meaning in our lives. Recognizing this similarity is at the center of true compassion. Instead of focusing on the differences between yourself and others, try to recognize that all these differences are just illusions. One of the best ways to get at this is to just look at what unites us.

Despite our differences and language, the way we choose to dress, the way we talk, and how we deal with certain issues, we all are driven by the same things. We have the same basic drive for food, water, sex, respect, protection, assurance—you name it.

Going even higher, all of us ultimately want to feel that our lives mean something. We're always looking for that great big "WHY?" Of course, we all differ as to what the answer to that question is, but it is still a universal and prevailing question.

Some people answer that question with material things. Others look at social acclaim and social position. Others focus on self-fulfillment and a sense curiosity or adventure.

The root of compassion lies in the things that unite us instead of the things that separate us.

In the 1940s, psychologist Abraham Maslow came up with a concept called the "Hierarchy of Needs." According to this school of psychology, humanity has several needs and all psychological emotional personality issues are really reflections of whatever dysfunctions we have in meeting these needs.

At the most basic, of course, is simple subsistence and self-preservation. You don't want to die.

But beyond that basic need is a need to do something with our lives, to achieve something. People have a need to prove to themselves that they are capable of making things happen; that they're capable of taking things they think about and turning their ideas into things they can see, hear, smell, touch, and taste.

Going beyond that is a need for social acclaim. It simply feels good to realize that other people are paying attention to what you're doing and rewarding you with validation. The highest form of this, of course, is love.

Maslow taught that the highest need is when we're able to finally break out of this prison of the self. When we're able to transcend and stop focusing on what's important to us or how people view us (self-centered pursuits), and focus more on universal truths like justice, fairness, kindness, and truly seeking others not because they are reflections of our own needs, but because they are ends in and of themselves.

This is the fullest manifestation of compassion, and it happens to be a drive we all share.

Look at someone you feel you have nothing in common with, or even that you actively dislike. Regardless of whatever hurtful thing that person has said or done, you share the same concerns at the end of the day. But they might be caught at the lower stages of self-centered pursuits.

Imagine what their daily struggles entail.

Now imagine that you're the one going through that suffering. Think about how much you would like that suffering to end, and how grateful and happy you would be to someone who helped you, or maybe simply paid attention to you. That's a feeling that can be developed.

If that person mistreats you, reflect on what their daily struggles entail and how they grew up. What kind of mood and state of mind is that person in, and what kind of circumstances are they coming from? How are they suffering, and in what ways can you give them the benefit of the doubt?

Hostile or negative actions are so rarely about you, and almost always about what people are going through themselves.

It's easy to lose sight of someone's positive qualities when they lash out at you, but when that feeling strikes, attempt to remind yourself of at least one or two positive qualities that you admire about them. Humanize them and don't reduce them to a single act that had nothing to do with you.

In the end, real compassion has nothing to do with you or your own needs. It has nothing to do with your gratifying yourself, making yourself look good, or feeling fulfilled.

Real compassion is when you finally break through the bonds of selfishness and self-absorption, and truly focus on somebody else's needs. You're not judging them. You're not condescending. There are no barriers. You're just accepting them and giving yourself to them.

Set your personal standards high in the form of compassion, and raise the bar for the people around you. You might be surprised as to how inspiring you can be. You don't have to turn into Mother Theresa - affecting one person positively is enough.

Chapter 17. Ethos, Pathos, Logos

Don't let the Latin in the chapter title throw you off.

The ethos, pathos, and logos are, like other chapters in this book, a different framework to persuade people to your path. It is a framework developed by the Greek philosopher Aristotle, and in one form or another has been around for thousands of years. In other words, it's proven.

This method leverages the three most powerful motivations people have outside of themselves, the ethos, pathos, and logos.

Ethos refers to ethical concerns, pathos to emotional concerns, and logos to reason and logical concerns.

Ethos and ethics

An appeal to persuasion by ethos is when you attempt to convince people on the strength of your character. The argument is that you are trustworthy and sound, and would never steer someone wrong. If your character is credible and trustworthy enough, then they have every reason to follow your lead.

"I've never steered you wrong in the past, have I?" or "I've done this a hundred times in the past, don't worry."

How do you make an argument about your character?

It usually comes from the past. Maybe you come from a good pedigree or you come from a very prestigious institution. You can also use your track record. Maybe you have shown that you are a fair and unbiased person who makes the right call every single time.

Maybe you've always carried yourself with dignity and class. The key takeaway here is that your power to convince the person you are trying to persuade revolves around your character. It can be your reputation.

Maybe you have shared experiences where people have seen you perform under pressure. They can see that you never lie. They can see that you never run away from a fight. They know for a fact that you always keep your promise.

Whether it comes from outside or from within, this method of persuasion is all about your character.

Appeals to character can only take you so far. Obviously, it does not work with people that do not really know you or with people with whom you do not really have a track record. It's limited.

Pathos and emotion

Have you heard the word pathetic? How about sympathetic? How about antipathy? All these words share the same root, which is pathos. Pathos is emotion.

When you make an appeal to emotions, you are by definition not making a logical argument. You are depending on being able to take advantage of someone's emotional instability to win them over.

One of the best examples is displayed in Shakespeare's *Julius Caesar*.

Caesar, of course, was murdered on the steps of the Senate by a mob of senators who were sick of his reign. He was not without his supporters, who quickly came into danger by association.

Marc Antony, a supporter of Caesar, burst onto the scene and was able to masterfully play the emotions of the murderous mob. He made it clear that Caesar's supporters were there to bury him and not praise him, turning rage into sympathy. Logically it would have made sense to kill all of Caesar's supporters to ensure that his faction was completely destroyed, but once pity and compassion entered the equation, logic left.

Marc Antony's speech is a powerful example of how an appeal to pathos and emotion works. You can either generate an emotional response in people to sway them, or you can capitalize on an existing emotional spike and harness it for your own purposes.

How do you make an argument that targets someone's emotions? By making them forget reality and logic. Use hyperbole and colorful, illustrative language that induces people to think outside the box of possibility. Craft emotional and intense stories to shortcut people's logic and engage their emotions. Make it personal to them, in a way that almost forces them to react in self-defense.

Above all, make them feel involved and affected.

Think about the television commercials that show sad looking dogs and cats in deplorable living conditions. They are the epitome of an appeal to emotions because they make you feel so personally involved that you act with a donation or adoption. These commercials are undoubtedly more effective than they would be if they simply stated the pros and cons adopting or donating to their organization.

More of our daily decisions are based on emotional triggers than we would like to admit.

Luckily, we are experts at justification and rationalization – we make an emotional decision, and then backtrack to rationalize it with reasons that may or may not be valid. We often let our emotions get the best of us, so we try to make it appear that we actually thought through our decisions.

Even if you feel your argument is dead in the water, you will be surprised how you can turn an otherwise slam-dunk case against you into a victory. That's the power of emotions – one of the most famous wars in (fictional) history began over a single woman, Helen, and her affections for two men. Is this logical? Of course not, but when honor and pride are in play, stakes can grow.

People don't always make decisions based on probability and the proper use of reason and logic. People are more emotional than they let on.

<u>Logos and logic</u>

Logos is when you try to convince an audience by using logic and reasoning.

Straight appeals to logic are very easy to see. You can see somebody appealing to your reasoning ability when they lay out an assertion and then support their assertion with facts. Truly brilliant argumentation breaks it down even further. They take the facts and then come up with different readings, either for or against their assertion, and then they knock down the objections raised by those facts.

There is a high degree of structure, and the argument almost reads like a debate.

An appeal to logos depends on the use of hard numbers and facts, and considers everything else speculative and non-determinative. Relevant comparisons are also used frequently.

All of the above is used to give the illusion that every piece of information has seen due diligence and is laid out in front. Logic dictates carefully analyzing the pros and cons, then making a decision based on them. Of course, this is a perfect place to use the situational framing we talked about earlier in this book.

An appeal to logos is what every other motivation attempts to pass itself off as. Some are obvious and transparent, but others are commonly mistaken and these are known as logical fallacies. For example, one of the most well known logical fallacies is an ad hominem argument, which disparages the holder of the stance instead of the merits of the stance itself.

They look as if they are making a sound argument by appealing to logic and reason, but in reality they are playing all sorts of tricks to prevent the audience from making a logical decision.

So which of ethos, pathos, and logos is best to appeal with? The answer is all of them at once, in a specific sequence. Human beings are emotional creatures and we have to be emotionally engaged – we have to *care*. The best forms of logical argument get the reader emotionally invested.

Therefore, the best use of ethos, pathos, and logos is to begin by appealing to emotion to draw people in and make them care. Emotions are the gateway. Next, frame the issue in a logical way that makes your argument bulletproof and infallible by dismissing the objections. Finally, your character is why people should listen to you and consider your words valid as a whole.

This is the basis of most sales and marketing, whether the salespeople and marketers realize it or not. It is also how you should position yourself as a leader – you are selling not only your path, but yourself to others.

Chapter 18. Connect Instantly

Your ability to connect with people is a reflection of your attitude. If you think new people or social situations are scary, guess what? Chances are you are not going to connect that well with unfamiliar people.

The key lesson you need to wrap your mind around is that your mental perception dictates your external reality. What you perceive the world and others to be will turn out to be the reality. The truth that we all need to understand is that we each have our own pair of lenses when it comes to perceiving reality and the truth. Everything that we sense is filtered through these lenses.

If you see through lenses that are very negative and fearful, chances are that your life will not be as pleasant as you would like. You will think that the world is hostile and not really a place of easy friendships and good times.

On the other hand, if you choose a different pair of lenses, ones that make you very curious and interested in how other people live, where they are from, and what it is like to be with them, you will get very different results.

You will notice that people like hanging out with you. You will find that you get invited to more parties. Life in general will be more fun or, at the very least, more tolerable. It's your choice.

Everybody has this pair of lenses. Unfortunately, most of us are unaware that we are even wearing these lenses. A key part of this mindset is, of course, our attitude. There are different parts to this mindset. It is composed of mental framework, philosophies, values, assumptions and expectations. But the biggest part is attitude.

Great attitudes for easier connections.

If you want to connect with people faster, more efficiently and more effectively, you only need to adopt the right attitude.

In fact, even if you don't feel that you have this attitude at first, you can start acting like you have it. Eventually, the signals that people give you will start reinforcing that attitude.

What is the right attitude when it comes to establishing quick rapport and personal connection with somebody new?

Think along these lines: I wonder what *they* are like. What can they teach me? What do we have in common? What are they great at and what can I learn from them? Ask yourself these questions. When you meet new people, feel the positive emotions that they carry. Make it your mission to find out everything you possibly can about them.

When you think about these attitudes, there's no reason to think they aren't true. We're not always the best at everything we try our hand at, and we're not all that and a bag of chips. Other people have at least five things that they can teach us about in a pinch — make it your mission and attitude to find those things and gain value from others, as well as impart your own.

Even if you are feeling apprehensive, insecure, have low self-esteem or low self-confidence, block out those negative signals and just let the questions carry you. By fostering a genuine sense of curiosity and adventure to push you forward, you can connect easily and quickly with people. This is all part of a good social attitude.

If you don't actually think that other people are interesting or can provide you anything of value (be it just information or entertainment), then you are likely to act that way and not establish any sort of connection.

Bad social attitudes to avoid.

While I phrase the good attitude you should have when it comes to social connections in terms of questions, when it comes to a poor social attitude, I'm going to describe it in terms of situations. If you find yourself in these situations, you have a bad or poor attitude when it comes to establishing rapport and connections.

If you go into any kind of social situation with a specific goal, chances are things are not going to pan out. Chances are you will project a poor attitude. Your goals put pressure on you to be social. When you are feeling pressured, it is easier to mess up. It also gives you blinders.

Yes, focus is sometimes good, but it can also make you oblivious to potential pathways for connection while in pursuit of that goal. In other words, because you're too focused on X, you miss the opportunities for Y and Z, opportunities that might have been extremely fruitful on their own.

Another situation that can lead to a poor social attitude is going in with expectations. If you expect to make a bunch of quick connections, chances are things will not turn out right. Instead of seeming excited and welcoming, you will come off as brusque, insensitive, or calculated and scheming.

This will also seep into the air that you project in your social situation – people with expectations act as if they deserve things, and as if they don't have to work as hard for them. People are more astute than you might think, and people will catch on to this attitude that you emanate.

Finally, one of the worst attitudes you can adopt is to go into any kind of social situation thinking that the people there are not worth your time. People easily pick up on this. People can quickly detect if you feel that they are beneath you. I mentioned earlier that literally everyone has worth to you, even though it may not seem like it initially.

You're also not a combination of Beyonce and Maroon 5, so why would you ever feel that you are better than others? If you feel that way, then that should be additional motivation to dig deeper and find out the interesting traits that others possess underneath the surface. Everyone is worth your time, and no one is inherently beneath you.

Best practices.

It is very easy to hit it off quickly with a random stranger. You just need to do one thing: give them your full attention. When you are in front of them, with neutral body language signs, give them your full attention, listen to them, look them straight in the eye, and essentially send out signals that you are welcoming and open to them; they will open up to you.

People are not stones that have no emotional resonance. We are always involved in a call-and-response relationship with whoever is in front of us. When you send off the right signals and give that person your full attention, that person will send signals back. This can lead to an upward spiral or it can lead to a downward spiral.

Try this exercise.

The next time you go out to a cafe or to a store, focus on working on your ability to establish quick rapport. You can do this by working with a member of a captive audience. I am, of course, talking about people who work at the cafe or store. The Starbucks barista or the store cashier doesn't have any place to go. That's their job. They are supposed to interact with you.

And the best part is they are required to be nice to you. So even if you fall flat on your face trying to make a quick personal connection, it won't matter because you will not feel the sting of rejection or mockery because these people are paid to be nice to you. Once you are in front of one of them, and they have the space and time to entertain you, ask them how they are. Ask them how their day is going.

They will give you certain answers. Be quick to pick up on certain answers that you can expand on. By giving them your full attention and focusing your conversation on them, you will be surprised how well you will hit it off. You have to remember that people love to talk about themselves. When you give people a forum to talk about themselves, they will take that opportunity. This establishes a great personal rapport and connection.

What happens if you screw up and the conversation goes nowhere? Nothing. And that's the best part. These people are paid to be nice to you. You can try again tomorrow, and the day after, and the day after that - until you succeed.

Above all else, imagine what the barista or cashier can teach you!

Conclusion

At this point, you might realize that you have far more toxic habits than you thought.

You might not be a Dorothy (from the introduction of this book) per se, but it's the small nuances and details that really endear us to others and allow us to handle situations in just the right way.

You also might have realized that Dorothy was thinking solely in terms of her self-interests, not making any attempt at empathy, and creating a decidedly unsafe space for me to share – as in, I never wanted to share anything with her again.

Often, we can achieve exactly what we want in a situation or navigate it expertly just by taking a step back and acting as if other people are three dimensional people1

Sincerely,

Patrick King

Social Interaction Specialist
www.PatrickKingConsulting.com

P.S. If you enjoyed this book, please don't be shy and drop me a line, leave a review, or both! I love reading feedback, and reviews are the lifeblood of Kindle books, so they are always welcome and greatly appreciated.

Other books by Patrick King include:

CHATTER: Small Talk, Charisma, and How to Talk to Anyone

Conversation Tactics: Strategies to Charm, Befriend, and Defend

Speaking and Coaching

Imagine going far beyond the contents of this book and dramatically improving the way you interact with the world and the relationships you'll build.

Are you interested in contacting Patrick for:

- A social skills, active listening, or confrontation fluency workshop for your workplace
- Speaking engagements on the power of conversation and charisma
- Personalized social skills and conversation coaching

Patrick speaks around the world to help people improve their lives as a result of the power of building relationships with improved social skills. He is a recognized industry expert, bestselling author, and speaker.

To invite Patrick to speak at your next event or to inquire about coaching, get in touch directly through his website's contact form at
http://www.PatrickKingConsulting.com/contact

Cheat Sheet

Chapter 1. Take Ownership and Responsibility

Taking ownership and responsibility over your people and interpersonal skills is the most important part of improving, because otherwise, you'll be expecting other people to help you along the way. And where does that leave you if they never show up?

Chapter 2. Find Secondary Self-Interests

One of the keys of understanding others is to take a second and think about their self-interests. Their primary ones may be relatively obvious, but if you can find their secondary self-interests, that's where you can really understand them and speak to their desires.

Chapter 3. The Anti-Golden Rule

The Golden Rule is off-target. It applies in a few circumstances, but encourages a self-centered way of thought. Instead, embrace The Platinum Rule as a rule of thumb on how to treat others. Step into their perspectives and get out of your own head.

Chapter 4. Reform Toxic Habits

We focus on what to do often, but we should also focus on what we shouldn't do. This is practicing self-awareness into your own toxic habits and how they might be repelling people, for example, if you are a conversational narcissist.

Chapter 5. Question Your Assumptions

We assume we know what people are thinking, why they act, and what their motivations are. We assume that we are mind readers and can accurately judge people. Most of this is wrong most of the time. Take a step back and challenge the assumptions you hold about others.

Chapter 6. Listen with Intent

Listening is an everyday superpower that most people completely ignore. You can either listen passively and nod your head a lot, or you can actively listen and participate – this is when you listen with intent and purpose and try to satisfy what you feel the speaker is trying to accomplish.

Chapter 7. Emotional Intelligence

Emotional intelligence is when you know what you are feeling and why – and that type of cause and effect intuition extends to others. The first step is to know yourself, and look at actions as opposed to words.

Chapter 8. Agreeable Boundaries

We want to be agreeable, but we often veer into doormat territory – and we want to set boundaries, but we might find ourselves veering into confrontation territory. There exists a thin line between being agreeable and setting up strict boundaries that you should sit astride.

Chapter 9. Open the door! Belief Police!

One of the worst tendencies you can possess is the tendency to patrol someone's beliefs and opinions. Think about agreeing to disagree more, and acknowledging the logical flow that led someone to their opinion. There doesn't have to be any logic.

Chapter 10. The Four Communication Styles

The four communication styles are aggressive, passive, passive-aggressive, and assertive. The assertive style is the most ideal and secure because it allows communication without subterfuge and ulterior motives.

Chapter 11. The Masters

Here, we examine approaches to people and socializing from prominent figures such as Dale Carnegie, Carl Jung, and Abraham Lincoln. Common threads include speaking far less and taking a bigger interest in others.

Chapter 12. Empathy Matters

In the 1970's, Patricia Moore conducted an amazing experiment that set the standard for empathy-based design

– a standard which can easily be transferred to other aspects of life.

Chapter 13. Workplace Tactics

There are specific people tactics you must emphasize in the workplace, such as conflict management, accountability, appreciation, and listening.

Chapter 14. Interpersonal Leadership
You want to strive to be an organic leader, not a leader by decree. You can do this by using tactics such as focusing on the success of others, listening with intent, and encouraging a two-way dialogue with two-way feedback.

Chapter 15. Handling Negativity

Frequent negativity from others can be draining, so addressing it as a mediator and helping others reform their own insecurities is a skill that will pay large dividends.

Chapter 16. The Art of Compassion

Perhaps nothing will help your sense of people skills besides simple compassion – recognizing people's struggles, accepting their actions, and understanding them.

Chapter 17. Ethos, Pathos, Logos

Different types of arguments and stances resonate with different people, so learn to cover your bases with the three main appeals: ethos, pathos, and logos – ethics, emotion, and logic.

Chapter 18. Connect Instantly

The impression you present is almost completely a reflection of the attitude you hold towards others internally. Do you *want* to connect instantly?

Made in the USA
Lexington, KY
19 June 2017